GROWING
SMALL
GROUPS

GROWING SMALL GROUPS

Floyd L. Schwanz

Beacon Hill Press of Kansas City
Kansas City, Missouri

Dedicated to my family—
my wife, Nelda
our daughter, Gayla, and Tim
our son Rick, and Kimberlee
our son Mark, and Sharon
and our grandsons, Bryce and Ethan—
my "most favorite" small group!

CONTENTS

I've asked Peter to give each of you a copy of
this week's discussion questions.

FOREWORD

We are born into the Kingdom one by one, but we are born into a *family,* have joined the *fellowship of believers,* and are members of the *household of God.* But what does this mean? How do we grow and mature in our personal relationship with Christ? Where do we learn to be Christian in the full circle of our relationships? Who will help us find our place and posture for involvement in the immensely complex social issues of our culture? These are serious issues—lifelong issues that we cannot handle by ourselves.

Thank God, we don't have to work them out by ourselves. We are part of the Body of Christ, and within the Body the Spirit is gathering small groups to share and pray and care. In them, persons are learning to love and minister to each other—to take seriously the business of becoming God's holy and mature people. Such groups are salt that preserves and light that illumines the world.

This splendid book by Floyd Schwanz makes clear the biblical teaching that our life in Christ is life together. Carefully he explains the need and place of small groups. He has spent years studying, creating, leading, and nurturing small groups in the church. Now he shares his vision and his experience with us in such a way that we can really learn what small groups are, why they should be, how they work, and how to get involved. He certainly creates "want-to" and helps overcome "afraid-of," but his special strength is in making plain the "how-to" for pastors, leaders, and sharing participants. I think it is an insightful book for folks like us who really do need each other.

—Reuben R. Welch

ACKNOWLEDGMENTS

Thanks to all those special people who have given me koinonia through the years in small groups.

Thanks to Mary Lou Butchart, who typed the first manuscript.

And thanks to Pastor Dale Galloway, for our friendship and for giving me 20/20 Vision and a place to serve in the exciting ministry at New Hope Community Church in Portland, Oregon.

INTRODUCTION

Often when we stand together in a crowd and sing about being in the family of God, the words initiate a personal thanksgiving deep inside us. But how *does* a group of believers become a family? How does the church become a community in the community? Answer: dialogue.

But how can we dialogue while sitting in rows and looking at the backs of people's heads? Answer: small groups. We *must* be more than an audience—we must rediscover what it means to be the people of God.

In reading the Gospels and the Epistles, it seems the basic launching pad for ministry was the small group, not the audience. Jesus invested His primary efforts in training the 12—a far different use of time than that of the modern church leader. The apostles also depended on the lay-led home groups to fulfill their assignment of "making disciples." It is not surprising, therefore, to discover that from the first century to the present, every great revival has been sparked by lay-led small groups and prayer.

Small-group ministry is certainly not a new phenomenon, nor a new church growth program, nor the latest "fashion" for us to buy and try. Giving opportunity for our people to grow in small groups is a very old idea and method. The Church born in the Upper Room did not have all the trimmings we insist our people must be given. They did have a life-changing message about a risen Christ who loved us enough to free us from the slavery of sin. When they proclaimed that Good News, it was personal and relational, more than facts and information about Jesus the Christ. Their message had convincing clarity, because it was directly linked to the joys and

11

challenges of their lives. And they rehearsed God's activity in them when they met regularly in small groups.

Of course, it was not the small groups that caused the Church to grow dramatically. It was not the small groups that changed lives. It was not the small groups that raised up equipped leaders. It was the Holy Spirit. The small groups simply provided the opportunity for growth, and the rest is history.

The purpose of this book is not to provide some more sophisticated methodology, but to assist those in leadership of local churches who desire a more personal ministry. My effort is to help you fulfill the call God has already given to your life's energy. My prayer is the same as yours: *Heavenly Father, I don't want just to live out my days. I want my life to count. I want to make a positive difference in other people's lives. In the name of Jesus, amen.*

Let's be honest now. Where, in most congregations of any size, is there opportunity to experience koinonia (the exchanged life) on a regular basis? A place to receive personal encouragement and instruction about personal concerns? A gathering where God's people can help each other with challenges in marriage, parenting, employment, societal issues, and so on? A forum where listening and caring and honesty and prayer and praise and study and burden-bearing and mutual support are the order of the day?

Most Christians have not experienced participation in an ongoing small group, and others just do not see the need. This book is an attempt not only to raise the awareness of God's people about the need for small groups but also to give tools with which to implement the ministry in a local church.

What I am suggesting on these pages is a very old

(and very effective) way of "doing church." When a person visits a church service that has its people meeting in small groups, there will be verbal and nonverbal evidence of God's life in that church body. However, don't be fooled by what has brought about that life. It's not the fantastic music and the dynamic preaching. It is the power of God at work in the lives of the people—people who are growing in their faith at least 10 times faster than if they were only attending another service.

How did we ever get to the mind-set that the Church of Jesus Christ is an audience? It is a *body*. Its health is determined by the health of the cells, not by how many people can be assembled. I guess the reason this is a little hard for us to understand is that we don't get to see all the Church at once. "Church" is happening all over the community at the same time in homes, lunchrooms, restaurants, and rooms in the church facility. And all of that life is hard to measure. This is especially true for those of us with a Western mind-set of church life. Small-group ministry is something we are rediscovering here.

In Africa, Central and South America, South Korea, and other areas, Christians have been experiencing the truth that "Small is powerful" for years. Before China closed to foreign mission organizations in the late 1940s and church buildings were converted into factories, there were approximately 2 million Protestants. It is estimated that today there are 35 to 50 million because of the effective multiplication of house churches.[1] And this is in a culture with strict regulations and a negative governmental attitude toward the gospel of Jesus Christ!

Have you read the challenging promise lately in Isa. 43:18-21? God says to stop rehearsing the stuff from the past. He wants to do something brand-new for our churches. Like making highways through the wilderness. Like causing rivers to break out in the desert. Like God's people having their thirsts quenched. Sounds almost too good to be true!

The conditions and the accompanying promise of Isaiah were very much like the time of Eli's priesthood. First Sam. 3:1 says that in those days the word of the Lord was rare and that there were not many visions. Sound familiar? Then hear the promise of 1 Sam. 3:11—God is going to do something in Israel that will make the ears of everyone who hears of it to tingle! Could it be that God is ready to do "a new thing" in our churches? He gives His promise to those who listen (young Samuel in 3:10). Are you listening?

The Great Assignment

Jesus gave us the command to "go and make disciples" (Matt. 28:19). We are to go to win others, who will become disciples, who will go and win others, who will become disciples, who will go . . . In this assignment, the words "go," "baptizing," and "teaching" are all participles in the Greek text. That means they derive their force from the one controlling verb *make* (disciples). Only as disciples are made can the other activities of the commission be accomplished.

Disciple was Christ's favorite name for those whose lives were one with His. John, who was a disciple, defines the word three ways in his Gospel.

1. We are disciples if we continue in His Word (John 8:31).
2. We are disciples if we love one another (John 13:34-35).
3. We are disciples if we abide in a fruit-bearing relationship with Christ (John 15:4-5, 8).[2]

I am convinced the small group is the best of all vehicles to get us to our destination of *disciple-making*. Without pages and pages of explanation, we can see the small-group method was the one Jesus chose. He had larger groups of followers, but when it came to training, He selected 12 to be with Him. How can we "be with" hundreds or 50 or even 20? He ministered to the hundreds from the small group as His base ministry. In a large group, people can be *told* what they should do and why they should do it. In the small group, they are *trained* by being shown and then by practicing such skills as applying the Scripture to daily life, engaging in intercessory prayer, reaching out to non-Christians, and confessing for healing (James 5:16). To tell people by our preaching and teaching that these are things they should be doing, without providing a way to do them, is cruel. They become overdosed on guilt because of everything they *should* be doing. They are frustrated with their Christian lives because they are so unprepared for ministry.[3]

If making disciples is really what church life is all about and if this happens best in small groups, then it seems to me that small groups cannot be just another program in the church's calendar. To make disciples seems to be the job description and the personal responsibility of every minister in the church, not just conveniently delegated to a staff specialist. To make disciples means to "be with" or "to come alongside" a few people until they can be raised up to do the same for others. Many preachers/teachers are trying to fulfill the mandate of Jesus by telling and telling and sometimes yelling. Disciples are not made from a platform—we need to get closer than that. To equip God's people for ministry (Eph. 4:11) is a whole lot more than giving them more information.[4]

15

Besides assuming that disciple-making is the responsibility of only a few, another condition that has paralyzed the Church is the idea that only the ones with an outgoing personality and upfront skills can minister. Oh, what a terrible mistake that totally ignores the doctrine of spiritual gifting! The clear teaching of Scripture is that every believer is given special ability for ministry. Having a spiritual gift is no common thing. It is something selected by the Holy Spirit (1 Cor. 12:11) just for us. Therefore, it needs to be identified and developed and used. Treasured and cared for? Yes. Raised up like a tournament trophy? No.[5]

God has formed and continues to form us into a *body*—with each member so unique and special. Each functioning member is as important as another. Just take a look around your kitchen. Do you see all those electrical appliances?—the blender, the mixer, the toaster, the grill, the can opener. Their unique functions are defined by their names, but do you see what they have in common?—the power! They each have a two-pronged plug at the end of a cord.

So it is with all of us. Resurrection power is ours (Eph. 3:7) to accomplish what Jesus gave us to do, but we each appropriate that power in our own ministry. As a combined result, disciples are made, and the Church experiences glory (vv. 20-21).

Are you a participant in a small group? Has your growth in your Christian faith been allowed to impact another person's journey personally? Or have you unintentionally decided to settle for a "business-as-usual" routine of church life? My desire is for you not only to be a part of a small group of caring people but also to help develop those same opportunities for the people in your community. And to that objective these pages are dedicated.[6]

16

PART 1

Conceptual

❀ 1

Biblical Priorities on Relationships

God in His very nature is "a small group." In eternity, before anything else existed, God was three Persons in one nature. Throughout Scripture we sense God's strong desire for us to be united with Him and with each other in personal relationship. When Moses was given the two tablets of stone, God outlined for us how we are to relate to Him and to each other. From the creation of humanity to this present day, God continues to love us with an everlasting love, calling us to himself in relational ways. The most significant of all, of course, was when He sent His only Son, Jesus, to make it possible for us to be rightly related to Him. God did not send an angel or a host of angels. God did not send a tract or a book. God did not send an organization. He sent a Person who had no human attractiveness (Isa. 53:2-3 and Acts 4:13) to impact those around Him in life-changing ways. And that's still His plan today!

Tough Questions

- How did we arrive at the conclusion that the Church is an audience, instead of a body consisting of cells?

- How did we ever decide that ministry happens best in a building, instead of through the lives of God's people?
- How did we give the meaningful ministry to a few who are professionally trained, when God has gifted and ordained all believers for ministry?
- How did we lose sight of the fact that we are members of a kingdom, and not just members of a denomination?

God wants us to be more personally bound together than most traditional church programs provide. Throughout Bible history we see large groups and small groups reinforcing each other, neither one being a substitute for the other. In the Old Testament it was the feast days and the family. In the New Testament it was the Temple worship and the house churches. We see the distribution of spiritual leadership in Exod. 18:17-27 and its sequel in Eph. 4:11-16.

From time to time it is a very healthy exercise for church leaders to ask themselves, "Why do we do what we do?" "Is this traditional, or scriptural, or both?" Cultural religion is a sort of malady, a trancelike condition that can strike any of us. We receive it from others and pass it on to the next generation like a family heirloom. When our relationship to God becomes only a habit, it loses its energy and its attractiveness. God wants us to live each day to the fullest in close communion with Him. That's why God sent His Son. That's why Jesus sent the Holy Spirit. God comes to live in us, and we have fellowship with Him and with each other (1 John 1:6-7).

The Jesus Method

The training program Jesus used was incredibly simple. It was built on His and His disciples' times of being together. Knowledge was gained by association before it was fully understood by explanation. Even today we would agree that one living sermon is worth a hundred explanations. Before Jesus sent them out, He wanted the disciples to be *with* Him. Like a personal guardian, He showed them how to live, how to pray, how to use the Scripture, how to teach, how to serve.

His method appeared to some as favoritism. Be that as it may, it's still the way He did it. He did not neglect the masses, but His method for winning the world was to call a few to follow Him. They were not in the prominent places in the religious system of their day, but they were teachable. Their most significant quality was their deep desire for God. Jesus staked His whole ministry on them, knowing that everything depended on their faithfulness after He was gone. Everything He did for the few was for the salvation of the multitudes. Evangelism is the genuine expression of God's love, and God is a *person*. Evangelism is real people reaching real people.

Briefly outlined, the method of our Lord looks like this:

1. He trusted them, allowing them to baptize very early after they had been with Him (John 4:1-2).

2. He sent them with a message and with authority (Mark 6:7-13; Matt. 10:5-42; Luke 9:1-6).

3. He empowered them to minister as though it was He himself doing it (John 13—20).

4. He supervised them with accountability (Mark 6:30; Luke 9:10). Like parents who love their children, we accept the burden of their immaturity until they can carry it themselves. We raise up spiritual children in our small group.

A wonderful illustration of the priority Jesus had on relationships was the model prayer He gave the disciples in Matt. 6:9-13. It was a group model: *Our* Father, forgive *us* as *we* forgive, lead *us* not into temptation, and so on. Even though this outline is very helpful in our private prayer life, it was given as a group model.

To emphasize how much Jesus wants us to be together, let's look again at the promise of Matt. 18:19-20. Two or three hundred being assembled is not the requirement. One person is not a group, but two or three or more who agree in faith have the power of God in their small group. It's not Jesus and me—it's Jesus and *we*. Two Christians are the minimum for community. For this kind of power to be realized today, we must shift from the traditional method of the pastor praying for everybody's needs to God's people praying for each other. Every time two people meet in His name, He is there, and the answer is on the way! The church that is ready to meet the needs of people today will be the church where people care for people in small groups.

The First-Century Record

One of the most exciting paragraphs in Luke's account of the Holy Spirit's work in the lives of God's people is Acts 2:42-47. I have always wished he had told us more. In only a few sentences he gives us a window into the Church life of the first century. When we identify the distinguishing characteristics of what was happening among those Spirit-filled believers, we quickly realize that those things happen best in a small group. It is amazing that in our modern society these things still happen best in a small group of committed and caring believers.

The assignment Christ had given was fresh in their minds. Their vision was clear. The power of the Holy Spirit was evident. But they did not build buildings for large gatherings—that happened 300 years later. They did not spend their time in committees, writing policy manuals about how to win the world. They had been commissioned (Matt. 28:18-20 and Mark 16:15-18), and they carried that commission out in both large groups and small (Acts 20:20).

An example of the early believers' method of augmenting mass evangelism with house groups is recorded in the ministries of both Peter and Paul (Acts 5:42: 10:24 ff.; 16:25 ff.; 20:20). Be careful—do not get the idea their success was because of their method. We read the Acts account and long for the same kind of church life. And the prophet reminds us again that it is "not by might nor by power," but it is by the Spirit of God (Zech. 4:6). Their focus was on their Lord, and with united focus they were in a true community of spirit. They were not doing it because it was doctrinally or denominationally correct. It was because the Holy Spirit was moving in their hearts.

With the same singleness of purpose as the apostle expressed to the Ephesian elders (Acts 20:24), those first-century believers moved forward because of vision. Without a vision, we can still go through the motions of church activities. In fact, it's easier to "do church" without a vision. All we have to do is use common sense as our guide—paint it so it looks religious but not be bothered with what God requires. They had vision and church growth. So will we!

The Gifting of the Believer

We firmly believe that God has given every believer special abilities for ministry. For what purpose? To sit in the audience and watch a program? No. Every believer is called, and everyone is needed (1 Cor. 12). Paul told them they were not lacking in *any* gift (1:6-7).

Spiritual gifts are not toys to be played with or trophies to be displayed. They are tools to be used in the work of the Holy Spirit. As leaders, we serve with the mandate of Eph. 4:11-12 to make God's people able to carry out their ministry. Therefore, we must recognize people by their anointing from God rather than by how much they know or how long they have been Christians.

I remember my early years of pastoral ministry—I had received a top-quality education, and I had lots of enthusiasm, but I didn't have a clue about my gifts. I just assumed I had them all, so I tried to be "Mr. Everything." In my heart I knew I wasn't, but I tried anyway. My people also thought I should be "Mr. Everything." After all, they were paying me to do their ministry.

What a happy day it was when I discovered my primary gift and identified the others clustered around that one! All were needed in the Body of Christ, and the other members needed me as I needed them. No more "Mr. Everything." No more "Messiah complex." No more "Lone Ranger" trying to take on the world. I am a member of a Body; I live in relationship with those around me. It's God's way.

While confessing, I might as well share another problem that arose while I was doing my best as a pastor. When I read verses like 2 Tim. 2:2, I was really frustrated. Paul told Timothy to select some who would teach others what he had been taught. I just didn't know how to do that—I mean, the reproducing part. I knew how to preach and teach but not how to get it to the next level.

Also, I had the problem of being a Christian who had never been discipled. I had Bible knowledge because of sitting in lots of services and classes, but no one had ever come along beside me to make sure I became a disciple. I knew I needed to disciple a few who could then go and do the same, but I realized it couldn't be done from the plat-form. It needed to be more relational than that forum. The larger a church becomes, the smaller it must be!

One to Another

If our living together in growing relationships with each other is less than a priority with God, then most of the New Testament could be tossed aside. The Sermon on the Mount is all horizontal stuff, and Jesus' ministry method was so relational. Throughout Acts we see God raising up a community of believers in each locality. The Epistles are filled with challenges such as the following:

- Love one another (1 John 3:11, 23; 4:11-12).
- Love each other deeply (1 Pet. 1:22; 4:8).
- Encourage one another (1 Thess. 4:18; 5:11; Heb. 3:13; 10:25).
- Serve each other (Gal. 5:13; 1 Pet. 4:10).
- Forgive each other (Eph. 4:32; Col. 3:13).
- Instruct one another (Rom. 15:14; Col. 3:16).
- Carry each other's burdens (Gal. 6:2).
- Confess your sins to each other (James 5:16).
- Pray for each other (James 5:16).

Those admonitions and many more like them can take place in a large group gathering, but it's not likely. Perfect attendance in church services will not provide opportunity for those needs to be met. Even though the church is a friendly place, the small group is God's design for giving and receiving "one to another." Everyone has opportunity to share in a small group (1 Cor. 14:26).

Life in Christ Is a Corporate Life

How can we find the Body life (1 Cor. 12:12-27) and the family life (1 Tim. 5:1-2) Paul described? How can we experience anything close to what the disciples enjoyed with Jesus? Certainly not by sitting among rows of people who nod and smile at each other but never share life! The New Testament picture of our life in Christ is a corporate life. Our salvation, without a doubt, comes only from Christ, but our ministry and our growth is a team effort.

Why do we see friends become dispirited and quit the ministry? Not because the work was too hard, but because they felt unsupported and alone. It's not a solo flight. We're in this together. We need each other, and when we win, everyone celebrates the victory. God has and will forever put a very high priority on relationships. In order to accomplish His purposes, He brings us into a synergistic alliance with each other.

Biblical Goals for Small Groups

There is a wide variety of groups God may raise up in a local church: neighborhood groups, specialty groups, children's groups, youth groups, task groups, and so on. Listed below are the basic objectives that are common in all small groups that meet to glorify God (1 Cor. 10:31).

1. Foster biblical love (John 13:35; 1 Cor. 13:13; Gal. 5:13; Eph. 5:2; 1 John 4:7, 11, 21).

2. Promote fellowship (koinonia) **and unity** (Acts 4:32; Rom. 12:5; 1 Cor. 12:12, 25; Eph. 4:3, 5, 13; 1 John 1:3, 6-7).

3. Build the Body (Rom. 14:19; Eph. 2:19-22; 4:11-16; Col. 1:10-12, 28; 2:6-7).

4. Nurture spiritual gifts (Rom. 12:6-8; 1 Cor. 12:4-11).[1]

The relational church knows how to celebrate family life. They are no longer content to sing the songs and rehearse the phrases about being the family of God.

They don't have to even think about it or try to act like they are family. They just know they *are!* Every week their small group meets, when they know each other better and love each other more. They share and listen, instruct and encourage each other because they are family. In this kind of intimate climate, new persons are able to humble themselves, confess their faults, and be healed as the "family" prays for them.

✿ 2

The Importance of Lay-Led Groups in Wesley's Plan

Church history records a New Testament quality of life whenever God's people have been committed to each other in small groups. One of those periods was during the Wesleyan Revival, both in England and on the American frontier. The class meeting was a group of 12 to 15 who met to promote the experience and practice of the devout life.

"In the atmosphere of mutual concern, it was possible for any need to be shared and for advice, instruction, warning, and encouragement in spiritual growth to be received. Since it served the dynamic of the people's needs, it became a real 'spiritual clinic' for the nourishing of hearty Christians in the growing Church."[1]

The meetings were personal, dynamic, creative, and cohesive. Spiritual growth flourished because questions were asked in a climate of love, such as, *What known sins have you committed since our last meeting? What temptations have you met with? How were you delivered? What have you thought, said, or done, of which you doubt whether it be sin or not? Have you nothing you desire to keep secret?*[2]

Attendance in a class meeting was required for

membership in one of Wesley's societies (which later became churches). Many historians are convinced the loss of spiritual dynamic in 20th-century Methodism was created in part by dropping the class meeting attendance requirement.

Procedure

The simplicity of the class meeting was profound. The group met weekly at a day and hour most convenient for the members. They began with singing or prayer and then gave every person an opportunity to discuss his or her state of grace. Each meeting was closed with prayer regarding the needs of each person present. An effort was made to keep the meeting alive by changing the procedure and varying the content.

The class meeting soon became the heart of the Methodist movement. It was in these meetings, rather than in the preaching services, where the great majority of conversions occurred.

Class Leaders

The minister who was in charge of the society (or a circuit of societies) made regular visits to all their class meetings to help them stay healthy. The leaders met weekly with their minister to give a report on their group and to receive instruction.

The class leaders quickly became an important part of the growth of early Methodism. To help them understand their vital role, James Wood addressed class leaders in a tract titled "Directions and Cautions": "The office which you are called to fill in the Methodist Church is peculiarly important. Immortal souls are committed to your care . . . and you are expected to inquire weekly how they prosper . . . and what progress they make in the knowledge of divine things. Much depends on your fidelity to God and to the members of your classes."[3]

Character qualities desired in class leaders were zeal, integrity, moral blamelessness, common sense, sympathetic understanding, and enthusiasm.[4]

Form vs. Power

One of the historical facts that has impacted me in a study of the Methodist class meetings is that renewal and revival did not happen in those small groups—no, it was already happening in the churches, and in the context of the Spirit's moving, the work of God was cultivated, deepened, and expanded in the groups. The revival atmosphere produced seekers who entered the class meetings. I'm not sure revival can be sustained in our day without small personal groups where disciples are developed with accountability and lots of love.[5]

The groups helped prepare for revival and conserved its fruit in irreplaceable ways. However, to organize small groups as a program method to revive a congregation would not be Wesley's plan. Wesley's small-group strategy followed, never preceded, the Spirit's leading. It is the age-old problem of trying to have the *form* (organization techniques) without the *power* (pervasive grace of God that changes lives).

Preaching Is Not Enough

The class meeting was vital in early Methodism, because meeting the needs of each individual was its main objective. The truth shared from the Scripture was applied by each one to his or her own life, surrounded by the love and encouragement of the group. Perhaps our churches have allowed God's people to be audiences for too long instead of urging them to share their lives with each other. Meeting together in a small "family" group is more important in a person's spiritual growth than to be optional, just tucked into a busy schedule "if there is time." In fact, toward the end of his ministry, John Wesley decided that his weekly sermon was not enough to meet the needs of the people. He asked, "For what avails public preaching alone, though we preach like angels?"[6] With this growing conviction in his later years, he accepted preaching opportunities only in churches that had healthy class meetings.[7]

The Decline of the Class Meeting

There is great speculation about the reasons for the decline of the class meeting among the Methodists. In America, between 1890 and 1900, the class meeting became generally extinct as the powerful instrument it once had been.[8]

I pray we can learn from these observations of several historians who comment on the decline.

1. With the arrival of a resident preacher and weekly worship services, the class meeting seemed unnecessary.

2. The role of the class leader in relation to the pastor was not sufficiently defined.

3. Revivalism brought people into God's salvation and the good life, but with "the experience" came an attitude that nothing more was needed.

4. As the churches became established, their thrust was no longer to the working class and the neglected population. With their new affluence and educational levels came less acknowledgment of personal need.

5. Many objected to the confession time with confrontive questions in the groups because it encroached into their individual rights.[9]

Old Method, Current Need

There is no question about the tremendous influence and expansion of the Wesleyan Revival in England between 1800 and 1850. One of the keys to its growth and power was the class meeting. There was such a warmth in their shared lives and mutual helpfulness—something not available while they sat in the midst of an audience.

Scores of instances can be quoted from Wesley's writings and other Methodist sources that praise this "providential act of God"—the founding and rise of the class meeting. Perhaps one of the best of these is in Wesley's letter to his friend, Vincent Perronet in 1748:

> It can scarce be conceived what advantages have been reaped from this little prudential regulation. Many now happily experienced that Christian fellowship of which they had not so much as an idea before. They began to "bear one another's burthens" [sic], and naturally to "care for each other." As they had daily a more intimate acquaintance with, so they had a more endearing affection for, each other. And "speaking the truth in love, they grew up into him in all things, who is the head, even Christ; from whom the whole body, fitly joined together, and compacted by that which every joint supplied, according to the effectual working in the measure of every part, increased unto the edifying itself in love."[10]

Charles Wesley expressed this dynamic best in the words of a hymn titled "All Praise to Our Redeeming Lord." The meeting-in-small-groups method is old, but the need in our congregations is current.

All praise to our redeeming Lord,
    Who joins us by His grace
And bids us, each to each restored,
    Together seek His face.

He bids us build each other up;
    And, gathered into one,
To our high calling's glorious hope
    We hand in hand go on.

We all partake the joy of one,
    The common peace we feel;
A peace to sensual minds unknown,
    A joy unspeakable.

And if our fellowship below
    In Jesus be so sweet,
What height of rapture shall we know
    When 'round His throne we meet!

❀ 3

The Vital Need for "Family Groups" in Today's Culture

Do you remember when a chip was a piece of wood, hardware meant nuts and bolts, and software was a T-shirt? We live in a world of many changes. Even the face of the family has changed. The word *family* once meant Mom and Dad and their children. Now there are 13 definitions!

We live in a culture with a declining loyalty to denominations. In fact, there are 100 million Americans who have no church affiliation. At the same time during which we are experiencing the breakup of the family unit and church attendance is falling off, we are still people who are searching for community. But where are we searching?

Someone has captioned our cultural maze with the words "You've come the wrong way, maybe." In the midst of value conflicts, it seems our churches continue to dispense quick phrases and offer programs that used to be effective. Today, as Christians, it seems every biblical comfort zone we have is being challenged. To meet those challenges, we need to change our conversation from *survival* to *growth*.

The world we have created with all our technologies is an exciting one, to be sure. But we can carry on our daily lives without making a relationship with anyone. With multiple channels available on cable television and videos of all descriptions, one doesn't ever have to go to a theater. Computers not only give us the ability to store vast amounts of information but also talk to other computers for us. With the use of our telephone and/or a catalog we don't have to shop away from home. And we can do it with a plastic card instead of real money!

We have developed a sophisticated system of transportation, with highways and shopping malls everywhere, but where is the sense of community? Where is the feeling of neighborhood? Have we developed privacy more than community? I think we have, but the pendulum is swinging back. Why? Because we are social beings by God's design, created to live in relationship with Him and with each other. We want to be part of the action, not just part of the scenery.

Cultural Needs

Perhaps the best illustration of how much we need each other was a popular sitcom of several years. It had a theme song that spoke of the need of people for identification, for fellowship, for understanding. Unfortunately, the setting for this song was not a church—it was a tavern! However, it does describe the needs we all have: to be accepted, to belong, to share life with each other. These qualities are not possible with strangers, nor among people who get together only occasionally.

Several years ago I supervised a call-in radio ministry at night from 11:30 P.M. to 1 A.M. Monday through Friday. We played positive, inspirational music interspersed with comments and prayer. We used the business lines at the station and had five phone counselors there each night. I provided them with notebooks filled with Bible verses in 17 different categories. When a person called with a need, a counselor could turn to that section and read a verse or two and then pray with the person about the need. I asked them to give me a brief report about each call so we could determine the kinds of calls we received and direct our ministry to help the most people.

I tabulated the results every week and noticed a very definite trend in the numbers from the most to the least. The order of concerns seen below in the sample stayed about the same for the 15 months we were on the air.

5,122 calls in 49 weeks
Average calls per night: 20.9

Illness (of caller or loved one)	1,185
Marital concerns	683
Problems with children (or grandchildren)	630
Stress	602
Financial concerns (or unemployment)	552
Enslavement to alcohol, drugs, and so on	530
Loneliness	484
Depression	346
Need of salvation	285
Church (location, service, times, and so on)	227
Bereavement	154
Psychiatric needs (emotional disorders)	137
Guilt	122
Feelings of worthlessness	63
Thoughts of suicide	51
Legal matters	50
Doctrinal questions	24

You will notice by combining the marriage and children categories that family problems ranked number one. The biggest surprise for me was where doctrinal questions ranked—dead last! With all the confusion in today's culture about our belief systems, I thought this would be more of a need. I learned that people need help with the hurts and the frustrations of life before we can help them with the foundation of their faith. What a mistake for us to turn the chart upside down and program our ministry with an emphasis where there is no need! Let's meet the real needs of people; let's meet them where they are by listening, accepting, loving, forgiving, and praying in heart-to-heart relationships.

Church Needs

Somehow the idea of making the journey alone and being individualistic in our mind-set has slipped into our church life. Have you ever felt lonely at church? There is good reason for you to feel that way: you are. Unless you are in front with leadership responsibility, you are just another face in the crowd—just another voice in the songs and the unison readings. You get the feeling that the service would be the same without you. Fellowship is what happens in the foyer between services, somewhere between the pew and the car (unless you've figured out a way to have fellowship with the back of someone's head!).

Somehow we have developed a consumer Christianity, and we already know that's not God's design. Try to imagine a family in which only the father talked. Try to imagine how the apostles could have matured in their faith if they had been together only for weekly meetings.

Relationship to God is a *we*. It's about time we take

some steps away from our overindividualized brand of Christianity and reach out to each other. I long to hear more *we, our,* and *us* than *me, my,* and *mine.* Reuben Welch illustrated our situation so well in his book *We Really Do Need Each Other.*

We Christians act
    as though we are deep sea divers.
Here we are in the murky waters of sin—
    but we have the protection of the diving suit of God
                  and
        we have the lifeline
    that goes to the great white ship up above.
You have your life in Christ
          and your lifeline
and I have my life in Christ
          and my lifeline
    and here we are with all our lifelines
        going up.

And we say to each other
    "How's your lifeline, brother?
      You got any kinks?
        Get it straightened out,
          keep the oxygen going
            or the murky waters of sin
              will come rushing
                in on you."
We wave to each other
and write notes to each other
    and we bump each other around
    and we say to each other—
            "Get your lifeline
               right."
            But here I am
            all by myself.

Once in a while someone gets the bends
  And we bump him up to the top
  or just cut him off
      and let him
         drown.
     That's not the way it
     is—
  because our life that we have with God
   is not just my life and His—
       no way.
I know this vertical relationship is fundamental.
I know that what constitutes us as community
    is His life given.
  I'm not saying
   that our relationship to God
    is not personal and unique.
    I'm saying that we are over—
     individualized.
You know what I'm doing
I'm over-exaggerating—
but not very much.
The
verti-
cal
line
of
God-
ward
rela-
tion-
ship
and the horizontal line of human relationship
are not two lines but one line in a continuum.
It all belongs together.

I'm not talking about what ought to be
    Or what would be nice if it were—
        I'm talking about God's reality
            about the way He has constituted
                the life we have with Him.
Our life with Him is tied to,
        is one with,
            our life with our brothers
                        and sisters.[1]

When the cares of life overwhelm us, we all need Jesus; but we also need each other. That's how His grace is delivered. In real flesh and blood we become Jesus to each other. I need you in my life, and I also believe you need me in yours. Together we are the Body of Christ, each member working in harmony and complementing the other's uniqueness. Now think about those nice words. How can they ever become reality for us if we don't spend some time together?

There are people who would try to tell you they know Floyd Schwanz. Don't believe them—they only know *about* me. They don't know me because I haven't *let* them know me. We've been together at various times and places, but we haven't shared life together.

In his book *Habits of the Heart,* Robert Bellah has diagnosed our society's problem as a disease of individualism. We are suffering epidemic proportions of loneliness and low self-esteem. We also live in a very mobile society with an increasing percentage of single adults. In an interview with the *Discipleship Journal,* Dr. Bellah emphasized the need for small groups:

Q. *What can the church do to help us become more connected and committed to one another?*

A. Small groups within the church community are one of the best ways to build "connectedness."

Small groups provide support. But it's more than that. The problems and pressures we face as we try to follow Jesus and understand what the gospel is saying to us are so overwhelming that we need all the help we can get in dealing with them. Hearing a good sermon on Sunday is certainly important; but it isn't enough. One of the vital roles for small groups is to provide us with a place to talk together about raising kids, making life's decisions, understanding stewardship, working out what we believe, helping one another, and learning from each other's experiences.

Q. *What do we lack when we don't have this kind of commitment within a small group?*

A. If our only connection to the church is that hour or so on Sunday, we become vulnerable to the values of the world: whatever is current, whatever is in, whatever the television tells us to buy, or whatever the beautiful people tell us to do. The amount of input from the church is simply too small to offset that. On the other hand, if we have a vital group experience where we feel connected to other people in a living community, that influence can provide norms, values, and direction so that we're not invaded by whatever the general culture happens to believe at any particular moment.

It's because of our constant temptation toward sin that we need the small group community—and the relationships that come with it—to point out to us some of the things we are doing that aren't as good as they might be. It's out of our weaknesses that we need one another.

Some have the notion that all a person needs is a good sermon and a few hymns, and then he'll be inspired to be a good Christian the rest of the week. Well, maybe if he's a very strong person. But for most of us, that's not enough. We need more. That's why small groups are so vital.[2]

One of the major reasons for churches to develop a network of small groups is to help people connect. Everybody needs to be connected. Disconnected people are lonely. We find life's meaning and purpose by being closely associated in meaningful relationships. When we become interested in other people and give of ourselves to them, we do not lose a part of who we are in the giving. We actually enhance and enrich our own personhood.

There's an old story about a man who went for a walk in the woods and got lost. He wandered around for hours, trying to find his way back to the lodge, taking one path after another but getting more confused and lost. Then suddenly he came upon another hiker walking in the forest. He cried out, "Thank God for another human being! Can you show me the way back to town?" The other man replied, "No, I'm lost too! But we can help each other this way. We can tell each other which path we have already tried and have been disappointed in. That will help us find that one that leads out of here."

Through Groups to God

A poem by W. Randolph Thornton says exactly what needs to be said in pinpointing one lonely stranger's search for love and understanding:

*Man's deepest need is to love and
be loved.
But man is lonely,
because he doesn't feel he can trust
his goodness*

and his badness
to his fellow men.
So he wears a mask of superficial
respectability
He tries to compensate for his
loneliness
by surrounding himself with
labor-saving gadgets,
prestige-producing possessions,
and attention-absorbing amusements.
But to no avail,
for man is not a thing—he is a
person—
made to respond and be responded to;
made for interaction and communication
with other persons and with God.
In loneliness man looks toward the church
hoping to find an alternative to futility—
a sense of belonging and of being wanted.
But often the minster is too busy officiating;
the laymen are too busy raising money.
Despite their polite remarks,
a stranger feels
they really don't want him—
because as a new member he might threaten
the smug complacency of things as they are.
So the lonely soul turns away
and keeps searching for the meaning of his life,
and the deep companionship of any
who will accept him as he is,
and give him a chance to invest his life
in a cause which will outlast it.
But all churches are not like this.
Someday he may find his way into a church

where there is a God-filled, redemptive fellowship—
where they treat him as a person with feelings,
where they look him in the eye
and really listen to him—
not just to his words,
but to the deeper longings from his loneliness.
Here is a church made up of small groups
of seeking and accepting souls
who once were lonely, too,
but are now engaged in removing their masks
and getting to know one another as they really are.
Their candor and frankness are refreshing.
This is what he has been seeking;
this is real.
The members don't act self-righteous, and superior.
They honestly accept him just as he is.
He doesn't have to pretend to be prominent
in his business,
socially influential,
or economically affluent.
Such things don't seem to matter to this group.
All they expect him to be is just himself—
a person, that's all.
He heaves a sigh of relief and relaxation.
In this free atmosphere
tension and fear are gone;
stiffness and formality have disappeared.
He feels a sense of release and creativity.
Here at last he can say just what he thinks
and still be accepted.
He belongs now—
not because he subscribed to a doctrine,
not because he signed a membership card,
but because he gave a glimpse of his inner life

to this group in confidence.
And they proved worthy of his trust;
they accepted him with all his loneliness
and inadequacy
and loved him in spite of himself—
because they felt that God had first loved them.
It was not a one-way giving, either.
The members of this group dared
to entrust their inner thoughts and feelings
and even their sins
to him, who had so recently been a stranger.
Somehow this group was different.
The members sat in a circle or around a table.
There was no leader, for they were all leaders.
They weren't afraid of silence, as most groups are.
They just listened,
and somehow communication was taking place—
a still, small voice was speaking to each
in the inner recesses of his own soul.
Call it the Voice of God;
call it the Holy Spirit.
New thoughts flashed into their minds,
new insights emerged.
All felt the warmth of a common understanding
and a new closeness to one another, and to God.
"This must be Christ's true church,"
he said. "This experience has magnetic power.
You can't keep me away from groups like this;
for where two or three are gathered together
in Christ's name—
there He is in the midst of them.
It is just what I needed;
my loneliness is ended;
I have tasted reality;

I know a group that understands me, and loves me.
As 'a member-leader' in this group
I can help in accepting others as lonely as I was.
I can share myself with them;
but more than that, I can share our Christ—
who would become their Christ, too."³

What are the basic needs of the human heart, Christian and non-Christian? Being loved and giving love. Being accepted and giving acceptance. Being forgiven and giving forgiveness.

The Big Deal About Small Groups

As the Church of Jesus Christ, the redeemed of the Lord, we are to live a life different from that of the world around us (Matt. 5:48; Rom. 12:2). God wants us to be holy (Eph. 1:4), and that means being different. I believe it also means going out and making a difference.

Allow me to share a few stories about God's people making a difference through small groups. The big deal about small groups is to go against the trends of our society.

1. A close family. This definitely would be the number one response if we surveyed active participants in groups. We meet regularly with a group of people who love us without condemnation, and we learn to love them. We forgive and are forgiven. We laugh and tell stories. We give and receive. We cry and hold on to each other when the going gets tough. We believe in each other, even when we don't agree. We don't go out and break the confidence of those who trusted us in the group. Every group who meets is a "family" who practices love in action. Every group who forms is another mark against the trends of our impersonal and self-seeking society.

Several years ago my wife was leading a group for ladies in our neighborhood. One of the members of the group was having serious health problems. Her skin color was changing from pale to yellow. The ladies tried to persuade her to get medical attention, but as a single mother without insurance, she was just hoping to get better.

Weeks passed, and the yellow became almost an orange. My wife received a phone call after she arrived home one day, and the lady was crying. My wife started to apologize because the ladies had been very firm that morning in insisting that she see a doctor. Her response was, "Nelda, don't apologize. I've cried all the way home because no one in my life has ever loved me enough to worry about me!" It had actually felt good to her to know of their concern.

One of the ladies took her to the medical school, and she was diagnosed with a liver ailment that could be corrected only with transplant surgery. The $140,000 was raised throughout the church in a miraculous way, a suitable donor was found, the surgery was a success, and in the course of a few weeks she was back in the choir, praising the Lord.

I had the privilege of being invited to serve Communion at my wife's group meeting when she returned. With tears of rejoicing, she thanked the ladies for their love, for the prayers, and for the notes she had received while she was away. Then she said, "You saved my life!" And that's true. That's not why my wife started meeting with those ladies, but that's what families do. They reach out to each other with God's love, and miracles happen in dynamic ways.

I remember the day I received a phone call from a frantic mother whose son had just been shot by a police

officer after he had threatened the police with a gun. I
went to the home and found members of their small
group already there, crying with them, holding them,
answering the phone, and keeping the media away from
the front door. They were like an instant family. They
prepared the meals and surrounded them during those
difficult days.

I was told recently about a single mom who missed
her small-group meeting because she didn't have
enough money for gas. They called, but she didn't answer because she didn't have the courage to tell them
why. After their meeting they showed up at her door because they were concerned. When they discovered her fi-
nancial need, they helped her get current with her utili-
ty bills, and the group who had birthed their group
made her mortgage payment, which was past due. Question: Who would you call if you had trouble in your life
this week? *Think about it!*

2. The application of the Bible to daily life.
Private devotions and Bible study are vital, but application is the goal. The group helps us discover and put
truth into daily life with accountability built in. Next
week when we are together, they will ask what has been
done with the truth we discovered. The finest sermon
ever delivered has one serious drawback—it is one-way
communication, a monologue. In the group we can stop
and discuss and pray at any point.

A wonderful brother in the Lord became a Christian in his adult years. He owned a taxicab and loved
having his Bible beside him as he drove. His customers
were curious and would ask him questions about spiritual matters. Because he was active in a small group,
he was always ready to share with them the latest
truth he had discovered. Many came to know the Lord

because the written Word became the living Word through his life.

3. Growth in personal prayer life. Effective prayer is a skill that is learned. We learn to pray better by *praying*. The group is like a laboratory. And what an encouragement to pray more when I hear of God's answers each week!

Because their children were in our Sunday School, God helped us reach a couple who had both been divorced and now were facing the challenge of a blended family. They were converted and began growing in their newfound faith. He felt the need to pray with the family, but his wife's daughter laughed at him when he stumbled around, trying to say out loud what was in his heart. But because they were in a small group, he learned very quickly how to pray, and she didn't laugh anymore.

4. Spiritual growth. The large-group corporate worship event is not a substitute for a small-group meeting, but the small group is not enough by itself either. Both enhance and enrich the other. It seems that as Christians we grow 10 times faster if we are active in a group rather than by just sitting in an audience.

I remember the morning one of my small-group leaders called to ask about how to help a couple who had attended their group the evening before. He said they talked constantly about everything but really didn't know the Bible at all. "What do we do?" he asked. Answer: Love them. The next week he called again with the same plea. When I asked what had happened when they returned, he said they never said one word the whole evening. He was afraid the group had somehow offended them. "What do I do?" he asked. Answer: Love them.

The couple returned the next week, and in the opening moments of the meeting the husband announced, "We don't know anything about the Bible or about living the Christian life, but we want to learn. Thank you for loving us and accepting us the way you have." It is no surprise that within a year they assisted the leader of that group and now for years have led their own groups, loving people and growing up together in their faith.

5. Sharing of life's testimony. Everyone has hurts and dreams, struggles and victories, questions and answers. Who can we talk to about our own joys and sorrows? When we share a sorrow, it's not quite so heavy. When we share a joy, the celebration is multiplied.

A lady in a Midwestern city lost her husband in death, and after God had ministered to her heart and brought comfort, she made an appointment with her pastor. She was privileged to be in a church that encouraged their people to meet together in small groups. She asked her pastor if she could start a bereavement support group for widows like herself. He said, "Oh, yes, and there is another lady who has talked to me about doing the same thing. Call her and get together and let me know when you're ready to start."

She called and made the appointment but got lost when she tried to find the address. Finally she stopped at a house to ask directions. The lady who answered the door helped her see how close she was and then asked, "What brings you over to this part of town?" When she told her, the lady started crying: "I'm a Christian and my husband just died a couple of months ago—and I'm not doing very well with it. I've been praying that God would help me. May I go with you?" Instead of a planning meeting that night, they enjoyed their first small group! It's really easy, isn't it?

6. Encouragement and edification. This is something we think about often, but we don't always say the affirming things we think. The group helps us stay up to date with our desire to say words that lift. I know in the years I have been a pastor I have depended on the love and the prayers of my people. But even though I know they love me, I still enjoy hearing them say it. Even though I know they pray for me, it's quite another thing when they pray *with* me.

I read in "Dear Abby" this testimony of what happens when we let God's love flow:

Dear Abby:

Thank you for printing the letter from "Feeling Guilty"—the mother who couldn't bring herself to show love to her 15-year-old daughter. I know exactly how she feels.

For the first four years of my son's life, I simply could not show him any affection and I was miserable because I couldn't do anything about it. Deep down I really loved Tommy and would have killed anyone who tried to harm him. Yet I held him at arm's length.

Why? Because I was crazy in love with his father, "Mike," who ordered me to get an abortion when I told him I was pregnant. (We were not married.) I considered an abortion, made all the arrangements, but couldn't go through with it at the last minute. That cost me my relationship with Mike.

I married someone else for all the wrong reasons, but that marriage didn't last long.

As time went on, I found myself being unreasonably hostile to Tommy. It got so bad that I actually gave him to a friend for a few days so I could get my head screwed on straight. After hours of soul-searching and praying, God finally spoke to my heart. He said, "You are blaming Tommy for being born and coming between you and Mike." When I finally admitted it to myself, it was as though a heavy weight was lifted from my shoulders.

Tommy is eleven now and I'll never forget one day about three years ago, we were driving down the street, and I just felt like reaching over, giving his arm a pat and saying, "I love you." He turned toward me, his big brown eyes filled with tears, and said, "Mommy, I don't remember ever hearing you say that before." Abby, that just about broke my heart. Imagine being eleven years old and never hearing your mom say, "I love you."

From that day on, I changed my ways and have said, "I love you" every day. And you know what? I really do.

No More Guilt in Illinois*

7. Effective one-on-one pastoral care. God never intended salaried pastors to take care of everybody. With a network of groups, pastors work with the lay pastors who work with their people. Ministry flows back the same way: group to leader to pastoral staff. Instead of asking the popular question, "How many members do you have?" we should be asking, "How many ministers do you have?" With a network of small groups who follow up on all the one-to-another commands in the Scripture, we can lose a major part of the guilt that plagues us in two ways: guilt (1) that the people we already have are not being cared for adequately and (2) that unreached people are not being touched yet because we don't see them in church.

---

8. Unlimited ministry opportunities. Lay pastors can build their ministry as large as they want it to be because of the multiplication factor. God blesses our faithful ministry as we "parent" new leaders and groups who "parent" new leaders and groups—and we become the proud grandparents!

About one year ago I was invited to participate in the memorial service for a lady who, alongside her husband, had led small groups for several years. Their groups never became big, probably an average of 10 to 12 people. But while sitting on the platform, I started counting the number of people who had come into ministry because of their faithful ministry. I counted 8 people—proving again that ministry makes it possible to outlive our own lives.

9. Friendship evangelism. The good seed of the gospel is sowed in fertile soil with a climate of love. That seed is cultivated. Coming to Christ is easy when needs are being met in a small group. Even those who have become hardened and defensive will sense those walls melting away when loved by God's people without judgment and condemnation.

Recently I visited with a pastor who supervises a number of small groups. He told me about an older man who has assisted in a small group for a couple of years but didn't seem to have the skills for taking full responsibility for his own group. In a leaders' meeting the prayer request was given about a young couple who could no longer attend their group because the husband was suffering with cancer. So this man visited the couple and offered to start a group in their home if they would invite some people.

When the time came a few weeks later to come to the hospital because of the pending death, it wasn't the pastor who received the call. It was their lay pastor, their small-group leader. While gathered in the hospital room before the body was removed, the young widow announced her husband's greatest desire was for his family to come to Christ. Six people committed their lives to Christ in those early-morning hours (including the deceased's father)! Praise the Lord—friendship led the way again to evangelism. And the instrument God used was someone who will probably never stand before a crowd and give an altar call.

10. Discipling of new converts. The best place to raise up a new Christian to maturity is in the same "family" that loved him or her to Jesus. It is possible to raise a child in a foster home (like a new believers' class), but let's not overlook the significant role the small group can have.

To continue with the above story, when I visited with that pastor again and thanked him for the story, he gave me the next chapter. With some coaching, the lay pastor was instructing them in the importance of water baptism. The date was scheduled for this public declaration of their faith. I wish I could have been there to see the pastor assisting the small-group leader baptize those six adults!

11. Creating mission projects. As needs arise, the group responds more quickly (and more generously) than a church committee ever will. Meals, transportation, child care, flowers, cash, and other items are provided that the church office knows nothing about. Giving God's love away is spontaneous and so creative when a small group knows the need and commits to taking action—not just at Christmas, but in the ongoing needs of the people around them.

12. Development of strong leaders. People become responsible only when they are given responsibility. People who are active in a group are learning how to lead without even realizing it, because it is a shared ministry, not a one-person show. I am convinced the best years of any church are the ones just ahead if their people are being "trained" as leaders right now.

Jesus has assigned us to go and "make disciples." That takes time; they do not just suddenly pop up in the church. I am convinced the best place to make disciples is in our small groups. Believers who are not ready to become disciples will be surrounded with love until they are ready for deeper commitments and growth. I am also convinced the small group is the best place to make "disciple-makers." In learning to lead others in a small group, they learn more about what they already know. And they learn to do it better because they keep practicing.

When facing the need for more disciple-makers in our churches, nothing (large group or one-to-one) beats the effectiveness of a small group. The small group has it all: teaching people to obey and moving them into ministry. At the same time disciples are being made, disciple-makers are also being made.

If your church is not offering opportunities for your people to meet together regularly in small groups, then how does your church provide for these 12 needs? Give the ministry back to God's people, and let small groups be the vehicle.

A Flesh-and-Blood Body

We must be careful not to get too sentimental about what it means to be members of Christ's Body. It is much more practical than we realize. When we feel that

God is distant, someone reaches out and touches us. When we sense a helpless wave washing over us, someone steps up to take us by the hand. When we confess our inability to cope with a problem, someone in an audible voice gives us a word of hope and courage. How childish for us to think that God is far away when He has surrounded us with a loving church family, a flesh-and-blood Body of Christ!

Just as Paul told the Romans in 12:4-5, we have a variety of members, each with a different function, but together we form one body, each member belonging to all the others. How it must grieve the heart of God to see His children sitting shoulder to shoulder on the church pew trying to tough it out! We *are* the Body of Christ, not just actors and actresses who are playing as if we were. As His Body, how would He have us serve? Jesus is here; we are His Body. Together we respond as He would to the people around us.

So I Stay Near the Door

Sam Shoemaker was one of the most remarkable Christians of our time. As a spiritual pioneer, he formed the seed ground of Alcoholics Anonymous and was influential in the forming of the Fellowship of Christian Athletes, Young Life, and *Faith At Work* magazine.

To him, people were "ever more important than things," and the most thrilling experience in life, he used to say, was "seeing somebody find Christ"—an experience that seemed to happen often to him. *Extraordinary Living for Ordinary Men* is a collection of some of his sermons. In the back of this small book I found his reason for living. It is mine too! I trust it speaks to you about the vital need for "family" groups in today's culture.

So I Stay Near the Door

An Apologia for My Life

I stay near the door
I neither go too far in, nor stay too far out.
The door is the most important door in the world—
It is the door through which men walk when they find God.
There's no use my going way inside, and staying there,
When so many are still outside and they, as much as I,
Crave to know where the door is.
And all that so many ever find
Is only the wall where a door ought to be.
They creep along the wall like blind men,
With outstretched, groping hands,
Feeling for a door, knowing there must be a door,
Yet they never find it . . .
So I stay near the door.

The most tremendous thing in the world
Is for men to find that door—the door to God.
The most important thing any man can do
Is to take hold of one of those blind, groping hands,
And to put it on the latch—the latch that only clicks
And opens to the man's own touch.
Men die outside that door, as starving beggars die,
On cold nights in cruel cities in the dead of winter—
Die for want of what is within their grasp.
They live, on the other side of it—live because they have
    found it.
Nothing else matters compared to helping them find it,
And open it, and walk in, and find Him . . .
So I stay near the door.

Go in, great saints, go all the way in—
Go way down into the cavernous cellars,

And way up into the spacious attics—
It is a vast, roomy house, this house where God is.
Go into the deepest of hidden casements,
Of withdrawal, of silence, of sainthood.
Some must inhabit those inner rooms,
And know the depths and heights of God,
And call outside to the rest of us how wonderful it is.
Sometimes I take a deeper look in,
Sometimes I venture in a little farther,
But my place seems closer to the opening . . .
So I stay near the door.

There is another reason why I stay there.
Some people get part way in and become afraid
Lest God and the zeal of His house devour them,
For God is so very great, and asks all of us.
And these people feel a cosmic claustrophobia,
And want to get out. "Let me out!" they cry.
And the people way inside only terrify them more.
Somebody must be by the door to tell them that they are
        spoiled
For the old life, they have seen too much;
Once taste God, and nothing but God will do any more.
Somebody must be watching for the frightened
Who seek to sneak out just where they came in,
To tell them how much better it is inside.

The people too far in do not see how near these are
To leaving—preoccupied with the wonder of it all.
Somebody must watch for those who have entered the
        door,
But would like to run away. So for them, too,
I stay near the door.
I admire the people who go way in,

But I wish they would not forget how it was
Before they got in. Then they would be able to help
The people who have not yet even found the door,
Or the people who want to run away again from God.
You can go in too deeply, and stay in too long,
And forget the people outside the door.
As for me, I shall take my old accustomed place,
Near enough to God to hear Him, and know He is there,
But not so far from men as not to hear them,
And remember they are there, too.
Where? Outside the door—
Thousands of them, millions of them.
But—more important for me—
One of them, two of them, ten of them,
Whose hands I am intended to put on the latch.
So I shall stay by the door and wait
For those who seek it.
"I had rather be a door-keeper . . ."
So I stay near the door.[4]

4

Seven Boxes to Escape

I was arrested several years ago by the title of an article in a Christian magazine, although I don't remember the content of the article. The title was "Locked in a Room with Open Doors." And here we are in the closing years of this century with a world of opportunity around us and church growth statistics that are pitiful to poor. In this chapter I am attempting to identify some "boxes" that have us bound, boxes that restrict our view and hinder our mobility. The seven are not listed in any particular order.

The Tradition Box

We have not witnessed a sweeping revival in the United States and Canada for a long time, but we continue with a business-as-usual attitude. We continue with our traditions as though they are still the most effective way to carry out our ministry. Wednesday evening services, hymn-singing from a book, Sunday School, and Sunday evening services are a few we hold on to. I am certainly *not* recommending a drastic move to throw out anything that we have done for more than 10 years. No, no. I am suggesting we see traditions for what they are—traditions.

There is nothing wrong with tradition. We must identify it and honor it, but please don't worship it. We need to hear our Savior pray again these words from the Cross, "Father, forgive them; for they know not what they do" (Luke 23:34, KJV). Even brand-new churches have traditions. By the time they meet the second time, they already have established their way of "doing church." Have you watched a congregation move in to a new facility? I have. No one knows for sure where to sit because they've never been there before. After they finally decide and are seated, you can expect to see them in the same seat next week (unless someone beats them to it).

We become emotional (and almost spiritual) about our traditions and don't even realize it until someone comes along and tries to change things a little bit. We don't even want the question asked, "Why do we do what we do when we do it?" But the question is an important one for a growing church. Traditions can be boxes. Let's be aware of them. Let's honor and respect them. But let's be smart about them. Let's avoid the box that says, "If you don't do it, you're not spiritual." Let's be sure we know the difference between what is traditional and what is scriptural.

How do we get into this box? How do we get so rigid about such things as service times and dressing in our finest, when those kinds of things have no biblical base? I am praying that we can get out of our tradition boxes by allowing the Holy Spirit to blow fresh, creative air into our midst. I'm praying for revival, that God will raise up some pioneers who will no longer settle for trying to patch up old wineskins.

Traditions are not wrong unless they are no longer God's will for His people. The Holy Spirit is creative, and when God's people are Spirit-filled they are filled with creativity. And I don't believe the Holy Spirit can be contained in a box!

Small-group ministries are receiving more attention these days but are not yet a common thing among us. Why? Partial answer: small groups are not traditional. Or we see what God is doing in other world areas through small groups, and we say, "That's cultural" and check it off. To deny our people the opportunity of meeting regularly in a small group is to ignore three things: the mantle of contemporary leaders, church history, and first-century Christianity. I am praying that more and more of us would no longer be content with services and classes (and more services and classes) while knowing all the time our people need to be challenged to grow up in their faith.

The Clergy Box

After His resurrection, Jesus made some statements that continue to challenge us today. In John 20:21 He said He was sending us in the same way He had been sent. Who is the *us?* Are the professionally trained the only ones empowered to do ministry? And have you read the translation of Matthew 28:18-20 from the Modern Version?

> And Jesus said, "All authority in heaven and earth belongs to Me. Therefore, men, who are 25 years of age or older and a graduate of an approved seminary, go into all the world and make disciples . . . and I will be with the few forever."

Of course, I just made that up! But I'm not too far off from the way we read what it doesn't say. We reserve real ministry for the professional.

> How did laity and clergy come to be seen as being so separate? One way to understand this is by looking at two Greek terms, *laos* and *kleros*. At first glance, one might assume that *laos* means "laity"

and *kleros* means "clergy." But we already know that *laos* means people—people of God. What does *kleros* mean? Does it refer to a separate group of people, an ordained group, comparable to our clergy? Not at all. *Kleros* simply means a "lot" or a "portion" or something—"a part," a selected part, a separate part. One might tend to think, then, that when the Greek word *kleros* appears in the New Testament, it refers to a select or separate group of people known as clergymen. Strangely enough, such is not the case. For every time these two words, *kleros* and *laos,* appear, they apply to the same people—to that portion of all humanity that walks with God.

As a follower of Christ we can all say, I am a part of the *laos* (the people of God), and I'm part of the *kleros* (those especially set aside for service to God). The separateness of clergy and laity was unknown in biblical times.[1]

The Reformers confronted the separation between clergy and laity, but they didn't go far enough. They tried to go back to the Bible and God's design for ministry. They took giant steps. But today the gap still exists. Strangely enough, we still consider the unordained as the uneducated and the unanointed. Oh, how that must grieve the heart of God!

When my brother and his family moved to Haiti, they enrolled in language classes to learn how to communicate with the people they love. To supplement the classes, they attended Haitian services (even though they are three- to four-hour events). My brother was complaining to a missionary about how much time the pastor used in giving the announcements. He knew the difference between the pastor's sermon and when he was giving announcements. The missionary asked, "Swanee, do you know the Creole word for Monday?" Yes. "Tuesday?" Yes. "Then next Sunday listen for the days of the week, because he is announcing the preaching points. His people cannot read, so a printed list can't be used. He is giving places and times and leaders' names for each day of the week."

My brother was amazed there were so many; how do they find leaders for that many groups from a church filled with people who cannot read or write? Answer: From the people God provides. The missionary explained how those leaders came on Sunday, already tuned up spiritually, to concentrate on what the pastor says. Without careful listening and remembering, they wouldn't have anything to say to those people who will gather around that porch out there that week. Is it any wonder that the church has grown in Haiti in recent years? Yes, all God's people are anointed for ministry.

When I graduated from college and entered full-time pastoral ministry, I knew I could do some things very well and other things not so well. But I did not understand the doctrine of spiritual gifting. I tried to be a "Mr. Everything" and hoped my people enjoyed what I was doing for them. What a horrid way to do ministry! I quickly found myself breaking one of the commandments repeatedly—the one that says, "Floyd, do not steal." I was guilty of stealing ministry. I was taking away from my people what was rightfully theirs. Rereading Rom. 12 and 1 Cor. 12 will help us get out of the clergy box. God wants us to work in concert with the Holy Spirit as our Conductor.

We need to get the pastor off the pedestal and back with God's people—different in function but not in status. Somehow we've trained our people that the pastor is the one who gets to do all the good stuff when it comes to ministry. That's a box that restricts what God wants to do in a local church.

Some pastors enjoy being on a pedestal because their weak egos will never come down. They will continue to do what they've always done—*everything*. How did Jesus do it? Answer: He gave it away and went so far as to say we would do *greater* things than He did (John 14:12). As a pastor, I must help my people become dependent on the Holy Spirit, not on me. Until that happens, they will remain followers, instead of the leaders God wants them to be.

It's always fun to list those ministerial privileges that are traditionally given to the professionally trained (if one is present in the group): Communion. Evangelism. Funerals. Public reading of Scripture. Planning the order of a service. Home visitation. Preaching. Leading group prayer. How did we get in the box that dictates only the clergy can do these things? Lay-led small groups will never be effective until we get out of the clergy box. Instead of staying comfortable with what we already know, we need a paradigm shift—with the help of the Holy Spirit.

The Fear Box

Fear may perhaps be the biggest box of all. It paralyzes us. It causes us to say more quickly, "We can't," than to say, "Let's do it!" The fear box restricts vision, and we already know what happens when we don't have vision (Prov. 29:18). The fear box also sets boundaries that call for very little faith in an Almighty God. We'll survey only five of the potential fears that need to be challenged.

1. We have heard the reports of the great success that has been enjoyed in the last 5 to 10 years in organizations that have used small groups to accomplish their own purposes. Cults, the New Age Movement, industry,

corporations, and psychotherapy have all benefitted by small-group dynamics. Since their motivation is different from ours, we run in fear the other way. We don't want to be shallow. We let their success stop us with a philosophy that says, "We don't want to do groups because *they're* doing groups." What a box!

2. Stories abound about churches that have experienced divisions when they allowed their people to meet in small groups. They allowed groups to meet, all right, but without being accountable to the leadership. So the groups become a ministry unto themselves, and God has trouble with them too. Sometimes the division comes when the people in the groups enjoy the warm personal fellowship provided there, and the church service is rigid and cold and boring. Stories about division can freeze us if we don't confront them with facts.

3. Many church leaders sincerely desire to have their people grow up in small groups, but they are tired. It all sounds like more work, and they don't know how to work harder and/or longer hours. Their energy resources are maxed in the same way Moses was overwhelmed when Jethro gave him the plan (Exod. 18:17-27). Moses discovered it wasn't working harder that he needed to do; it was working *differently*.

4. Shifting gears and moving into an unknown area is always going to raise our anxiety levels. Many church leaders have never been a part of an ongoing relational small group, let alone led one. I have heard humorous stories about pastors who tried to lead a small group in a home but couldn't sit down when they did it. Can you imagine how intimidating that was for the people sitting there? The man was taught to preach and teach the Bible, not to lead a discussion. Professional? Yes. Relational? No. They've never learned how to make themselves

vulnerable. Therefore, they are lonely because they never share their own stuff. Fear of the unknown is a box. I long to hear more pastors refer to "my small group." I pray for church leaders who can find a group of people to love and who will love them, where they can be honest and share life in a small group instead of an audience.

5. A very definite societal thing has slipped into our churches—the fear of intimacy. Have you noticed a person looking for a place to sit in the gate area of an airport? They finally choose a seat as far from another person as possible. Not so in other cultures. You'll find them clustered in one bunch, with empty seats all around the edges. And we wonder why our people fear intimacy.

In my first pastorate, I tired of trying to do another little sermon on Wednesday evening at the church, preceded by stiff little prayers. I wanted it to be more relational, so I took my screwdriver on Wednesday afternoon one week. I unfastened the front pew from the hardwood floor and turned it around, facing the back of the chapel. The second pew was put against the outside wall. The third pew was placed on the center aisle. The fourth pew was left in place so the 15 to 20 who came could see each other and talk to each other.

But as soon as they arrived, I knew I was in trouble. They sat down all right—and glared at me! They didn't want to talk to each other or pray for each other and get real. They were afraid to say something like, "I'm not doing very well. Please pray for me."

Needless to say, on Thursday morning I fastened the pews back where they belonged. I learned how *not* to do it. I didn't know what I know now about small-group ministries. I witnessed the fear of intimacy among people who really did care for each other.

How can church leaders escape the fear box? Answer: Face up to fear with turned-on faith!

The Control Box

I'll never forget a conversation I once had with a district superintendent about how successful pastors are flexible when it comes to methodology. His illustration was of a basketball coach who had enjoyed a winning program built on a fast-break style of play. What happens when he moves to a new school and the team that turns out is tall and on the heavy side? They can put the ball into the hoop, but they can't spring like his former teams. If he doesn't teach them a half-court offense, he probably won't have a winning season. His previous method needs to be replaced. It worked there, but it won't work here. To say, "This is the way it has to be," is a control issue. The principle is this: *Growing churches are flexible*—not in theology, but in methodology.

A few years ago I was consulting with a pastor who had grown his small-group ministry from 2 to 20 in two years but continued to face more than a little opposition. God was doing miraculous things in the groups, but group life had not touched his older people. Some of them were on his board and were very verbal about their displeasure over all the groups that were springing up and led by people they didn't even know. They felt the board should be approving each one—even though they didn't know much about what actually happened in the groups.

In the conversion it suddenly dawned on us what the real problem was: control. The church board has control over two major items: the budget and the building. Our small-group leaders are volunteers who use a discussion guide the pastor provides, so they need no money. The groups meet in homes, so they are not on the facility schedule. Can you see the scenario? The decision-makers had lost control! God was blessing the church in multiplied ways, and they couldn't stop it. Praise the Lord! To help them get out of the control box, I suggested to the pastor that he include some nurture time in his board agenda, helping them learn to care for each other.

Low self-esteem in church leaders also will keep them in the control box. They are not strong enough emotionally to handle other people's success and recognition. They cannot imagine what it would be to have so many good things happening in multiplied groups, when they knew they couldn't be in every one to make sure they did it right.

This reminds me of what happened to the buffalo herds in early America. They were decimated because the hunters discovered that their vulnerability was in getting the head buffalo down. If they could get him, the rest of the herd stood around, not knowing what to do. They were easily slaughtered.

This principle also applies to my family. As a father I need to lead my family but avoid the "command and control" style of the head buffalo. I want my wife and children to be able to make good decisions on their own—away from me. I want to be their leader but not their boss. A leader empowers followers; a boss holds onto the power. A leader encourages creativity; a boss always wants the last word. A leaders trusts; a boss distrusts.

Control is a box. Pastors try to control churches; churches try to control pastors. Jesus is Lord. That means He has the authority on His side, but He trusts *us* with *His* ministry.

Just for fun, I asked a roomful of pastors to raise their hands if they believed in the Holy Spirit. Every hand went up, just as I expected. Then I asked the bigger question: "Do you trust the Holy Spirit? Do you trust the Holy Spirit to anoint those small-group leaders and to perfectly orchestrate what happens in their group?" Well, they hesitated. Not every hand went up. I appreciated their honesty.

To get out of the control box we need to realize we cannot make people do *any*thing. Basically, there are two ways to motivate our people: by fear or by love. Both are successful; both will produce results.

Fear is a very effective motivator. Guilt trips and threats (even bribes) will get results, but only for the short term. I don't recommend fear motivation—that's control.

Love is a very effective motivator. That's the one Jesus chose. That's the one that brings out the best in me. That's the one my mother-in-law used the first time I dated my wife. I asked her when I should have Nelda back home, and she said, "Whenever you think is best." No mother had ever said that to me before. She trusted me, and I can testify that was a positive motivation. I was a good boy that night and actually had her daughter home earlier than normal.

It was Christmastime, and lots of shoppers were in the store when the little boy bumped into a pyramid of shoe boxes at the end of an aisle. Shoes and boxes and tissue paper went everywhere. The manager was already stressed, and now this. With his hands on his hips he was yelling, "Pick them up! Pick up every one! And make sure the pairs match!" The little boy started crying, and his older sister knelt down beside him and started picking them up. He joined in to help her. As everyone watched, she looked up at the manager and said, "Mister, you've got to *love* him into doing it."

The Curriculum Box

This is a very popular box, because we come from an academic point of view. But, having the right material will not assure the success of the group. That's a box from which we must escape. From our own schoolroom experiences, we already know the difference between the good experiences and the poor ones. And it isn't the textbooks—it's the enthusiasm of the teachers about the subject, and their ability to relate to us. In small groups, we transfer faith to others with our lives more than with our lessons.

The reason we come together each week is to exchange life (koinonia) and help each other grow. Yes, we have a lesson, but it is only a vehicle to help us meet the needs of our people. We must get out of the box that says we have a good meeting if we have the right lesson.

The best discussion guide is going to be the simple one of five or six questions provided by the pastor. The questions are personal and help us make application of a Scripture passage to our daily lives. There is a wide variety of group lessons available for purchase. Buy them and rewrite them. Chapter 13 will help you become proficient. Emphasize what you want to emphasize, and throw out what doesn't seem to fit. When the local church name is used here and there, our people will know no one else is doing that lesson. It has come from the pastor and therefore is special.

Small-group ministry is a relationship ministry. It is the connecting of our people with each other and with the Holy Spirit. How important is the curriculum when the Holy Spirit comes into a group? Melting hearts.

Opening hearts. Strengthening weak hearts. Causing love to flow.

The Guilt Box

Have you never overdosed on guilt? I have many times. It takes various forms, and I'll list only a few. Guilt is a box that certainly hinders the development of small groups.

Many church leaders testify of failure in the past when they tried small groups and they didn't fly. Their conversation is filled with words like "shoulda" and "coulda." Looking back is good for us if we are teachable. Learn from past failures and move on. Don't get stuck in the guilt box.

Sometimes we feel guilty when we look around and see only what we don't have instead of what we do have. I have always wanted more growth where I have pastored than what I have recorded. But I cannot be effective *today* if I let our lack of growth in the past whip me. It ruins me for today if I feel I've failed God and missed His best in my life. When I get down like that, I'm no fun to live with for my family either! All of us can testify, "I have failed." But we can also say with confidence, "I am not a failure," because God is not finished with me yet. It is easy to get stuck in the guilt box, but we don't have to stay there.

We also feel guilty when we start recruiting leaders for our groups. We see our faithful people who are already overcommitted and overworked. How can we ask them to do anything more? Wow, what a guilt trip! As church leaders, we need to give permission to our leaders to say a positive no to good things without apology. Take away their guilt as they decide not to do some things in order to lead a small group. Take away their guilt if they decide to do other things instead of leading a small group. The choices we have to make are not always easy. It is easy for me to choose between the good and the bad, but not so easy when I must decide between the best and the good.

In one day there are 10 things I want to do, but I know I cannot do 10 things. I can do about 3. So I must choose 3 from the list of 10. To decide not to do the other 7 is the hard part. However, if I don't let go of the 7, I cannot give my best to the 3.

One other source of guilt: all those "one to another" verses. They have been given to me in the Scripture to encourage me, but they have the potential of producing guilt. When I know of people in our church family who are not being cared for, the guilt begins to mount. When I know of people in our community who are not being touched with God's love, I feel guilty for not reaching out as I know I should. To get myself out of that guilt box, I give my energy to small groups and my leaders, because they are the best way I have of helping our people connect.

The Department Box

This is the most subtle of the seven boxes. We are surrounded with departmental organizations: local, state, and federal government; corporations; retail businesses; public education; and even Christian education. So it's only natural for us to form small-group ministry as another department in the church. A survey of churches in America who do have small groups revealed that 80 percent of them have a departmental system. They have a youth person, a music person, a Sunday School person, a children's person, an evangelism person, a visitation person, and now a small-group person. When that happens, something as important as group life has just been departmentalized instead of being an integral part of church life as it was in the first century. Good things will happen in those groups, but as long as they are part of a "department," they will only remain as another option for the people—one more choice on the multiple choice list.

To begin escaping the department box, I suggest starting with the staff meeting. It doesn't matter if the staff is salaried or volunteer—the leaders need to be in a nurture group. By their own experience they will learn how to build their own ministries with small groups. Instead of a department in the church, the church will have a totally integrated system. Every group that meets regularly for whatever reason will be an opportunity for the people to care for each other.

Obviously, it would not be appropriate suddenly to jerk people out of this box. It takes time to change a system. Change the concept of church life, and *then* change the organization. To announce to a church that their existing program is going to cease and desist and be replaced by a new program would be too drastic, to say the least. Some churches are just not ready for small groups. But they can be if their leaders will get God's vision and plan a strategy with lots of patience. Let love lead the way, and changes will occur. The Holy Spirit guarantees that!

PART **2**

Practical

5

How to Organize
an Ongoing System,
Not Just Another Ministry

All the benefits of a small-group ministry described in this book are only part of a dream if we continue to think of it as installing another program. Small groups are receiving new attention these days, and church leaders are tempted to think in terms of "Oh! Small groups? What a great idea! Let's start some small groups. We're not having much success in anything else right now— let's try small groups." So they buy another notebook and some tapes, take them home, and try to recruit a few uninvolved people or some who say yes to everything and behold: another ministry.

Even churches who are seriously considering a small-group ministry will discover a wide variety of small groups already meeting. Most will be together primarily to perform a task, such as music, athletics, committees, boards, prayer, senior adults, and ushers/greeters. But if the leaders are visionary, they will encourage *all* groups to move up on the nurture scale. This investment, added to the development of the groups described in this book, will pay huge dividends in the future life of the church.

When the relational ministry provided in small groups is seen as the New Testament design for God's people, it will affect everything else the church does. This is far different from trying to crowd small groups into an already busy calendar. When (and until) lay-led small groups become the vision and the heart of the church leaders, they will never be a priority for the church body.

Smaller churches will be revived when a network of groups does the major part of pastoral care, making it possible for a bivocational pastor to do more real ministry than a full-time pastor without small groups. Larger churches will continue to grow larger when they meet the needs of their people through a network of dedicated lay pastors. Churches can grow large enough to impact a city, small enough to care.[1]

Small Groups in the Total Life of the Church

All of us have three needs as we build our faith. All three ministry opportunities are provided by our church. Obviously, as illustrated, we can expect overlaps, because the Bible is our only authority in each one, and the leaders use spiritual gifts in each of the three.

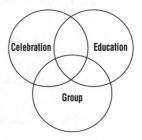

Celebration is our opportunity for corporate worship and praise. Yes, there is teaching when we are in this large-group event, but it is not a giant classroom. Yes, there is also fellowship, but it's very difficult to get acquainted while sitting in rows.

Education is our opportunity for serious and stimulating teaching. Yes, there is a worship atmosphere. Yes, there is also fellowship, but this is a classroom with a teacher/student dynamic that is content-oriented.

The **Group** is our opportunity to experience koinonia—the sharing of life in the fellowship God wants for His people. Yes, there is worship and praise, but this is not a mini church service. Yes, there is teaching, but a group is life-centered rather than lesson-centered.

Repeated in Acts and the Epistles are references of large groups and small groups meeting regularly. Perhaps the best summary is in Paul's farewell to the Ephesian elders: "I have not hesitated to preach anything that would be helpful to you but have taught you publicly *and* from house to house" (Acts 20:20, emphasis added).

All of us have these three basic needs in order to grow up in our faith. We need to worship with God's people, we need to study God's Word, and we need to share our lives with each other. Services are designed for worship; classes are designed for study; small groups are designed for the sharing of life. Without having clear objectives, we tend to do the same thing each time we meet.

So which one is the most important—the large group, the class, or the small group? That's like asking which of my three children I love the most. I cannot answer that, because they are not in competition. We need the corporate worship event *and* the small-group fellowship, as well as the serious study. *Each one serves to reinforce the other two.*

This book provides a strategy to satisfy the need we have in the Christian community to care and be cared for. Small relationship groups happen to be the one ministry most churches neglect. This will be a tool for them. Now, with past-due attention, small-group ministries are growing—and growing in many dimensions. Sound like Acts 29?

Churches that catch the vision and develop a strategy for small groups will strengthen both their inreach and their outreach. Other churches will be like the old elephant who has been chained to an iron stake since his youth. He now has the strength to pull up that stake and walk away, but he doesn't have the mind-set.

Why Every Church Needs a Small-Group System

Here are the reasons every church needs a small-group system:

- *To provide multiple points of entry into the influence of the church.* Sunday services are not enough. Big events are not enough. We need to provide meaningful ministry where the people are—away from the church!
- *To impact more people with the claims of the gospel.* For whatever their reasons, the very people we need to reach are not streaming into the church. Loving them where they are makes evangelism effective. The ministry of Jesus was relational.
- *To care for the personal needs of the people we already have.* This can never be accomplished by a few salaried professionals. That was not and is not God's design. Ministry flows from the staff through the leaders to the people and back again.
- *To accelerate spiritual growth in our people.* Gifts

for ministry are discovered and developed. Disciples and disciplers are both raised up in small groups.

- *To shift the work of the ministry to God's people, with their leaders resourcing them.* This would fulfill Eph. 4:11-12 and result in 4:13-16.[2]

A Simple Organization

The organization needed for a network of small groups in the life of a church is a rather simple one— even if we are called on to care for hundreds or thousands of people. It is the same plan Jethro gave his son-in-law, Moses, in Exod. 18:17-27. Four problems are identified that sound so contemporary:

- Moses was exhausted because he was overwhelmed at trying to do it alone.
- The people were complaining because their needs were not being met.
- Leaders were unfulfilled because their abilities were not being used.
- There was an unhealthy dependence on Moses (Exod. 18:14).

Basically, the plan suggested to him was to give away what he had assumed was all his. Jethro told him his people could judge how much they could handle, and the difficult cases would be brought to him. Give Moses credit for listening and because he followed the counsel, all the people went home satisfied (18:23). Moses probably had a good night's rest too.

The New Testament sequel of this principle is found in Eph. 4:11-13, where the apostle says God's people do the ministry as they are equipped by their pastors. To equip means to "make able," the same word used in Matthew and Mark in reference to the mending of

nets—making the nets able to do what they were designed to do. Pastors help make God's people able to do
what they were designed to do.

In the system we have developed where I serve, it
looks like this. Notice that we have used the strong
principle of coaching from this passage to structure our
ministry like the one in Exodus.

- One lay pastor cares for about 10 people.
- One lay pastor captain cares for 5 lay pastors (or 50 people).
- One lay pastor coach cares for up to 10 lay pastor captains (who have 50 people each).

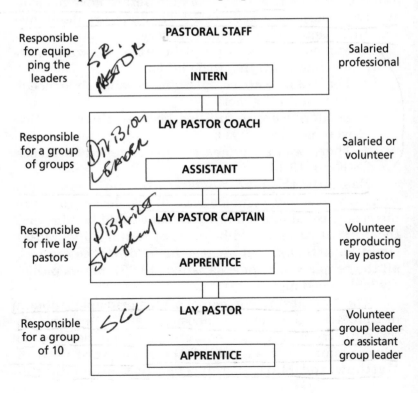

Responsible for equipping the leaders	**PASTORAL STAFF** **INTERN**	Salaried professional
Responsible for a group of groups	**LAY PASTOR COACH** **ASSISTANT**	Salaried or volunteer
Responsible for five lay pastors	**LAY PASTOR CAPTAIN** **APPRENTICE**	Volunteer reproducing lay pastor
Responsible for a group of 10	**LAY PASTOR** **APPRENTICE**	Volunteer group leader or assistant group leader

- One pastor cares for all the lay pastor coaches, who care for everybody else.

The previous page illustrates a more familiar organization chart.

Notice: At each level of leadership there is someone in training, someone who is learning to do what the leader does. This provides a built-in multiplication factor.

Three Small-Group Systems

Every small-group ministry can be identified in one of three systems. Some are categorized as an *appendage system.* They are lay-led and most often were lay-initiated. They continue to function with little or no staff support or recognition. They are like an arm or a leg of the body—connected, but just kind of "out there." Most of the churches in North America that do have small groups have a *department system.* A staff person supervises their ministry, and although the senior pastor considers participation to be important, small groups are just another choice in the church's activity schedule. The third type is on the increase. It is the *integrated system.* All staff members are "coaching" lay leaders and supervising their groups. Evangelism and disciple-making is happening throughout every ministry of the church as God's people meet in small groups. In churches that *a little high* have adopted an integrated system, 80 to 90 percent of their people will be involved in small groups. And the best years for those churches are just ahead, because of all the life the groups are generating and the leaders who are being raised up.[3]

The most attractive element in an integrated system is how growth is sustained. Once a church has this system in place, every ministry is built with small groups. When enough groups are developed in any ministry, they can move on under a "coach" and continue growing without going through change. Out of a few neighborhood groups, a group for young singles and a couple of ladies' groups are born. Before long, more singles' groups and more ladies' groups are formed until both are strong ministries, each with a supervising pastor who helps them grow. Oh, how different that is than trying to convince a group of singles and/or ladies that they need a new program!

Jesus Gave Himself

Jesus' life was one of giving, not an experiment to take home and try for 10 days. He gave what the Father had given Him. He gave His disciples His peace. He gave them His joy. He gave them the keys of the Kingdom. He gave them His own glory. He gave His own life. And that's love—giving of self to others.

Basically, there are about six areas of ministry that every local church wants to provide as we give God's love away:

- Worship
- Teaching/preaching
- Discipleship
- Evangelism
- Fellowship (inreach and outreach)
- Administration of pastoral care

I am convinced that all except worship and teaching/preaching happen best in a small group led by believers who are committed to God's high calling of healing hurts and building dreams. But instead of picking up the mantle from church leaders like Wesley and others, along with the model of the first-century Church, we keep doing services and classes—and more services and classes, knowing all the time that our people need to be challenged in more personal ways to grow up in their faith, a dimension of maturity not possible as long as they are content to be in someone's audience.

The Pastor's Role

Once a pastor has decided that God's design for the local church includes the opportunity for people to meet together regularly in small groups, he or she then needs to stay in a central place of leadership. Not that the pastor does everything for everybody else, but if small-group ministry is not a priority in his or her own schedule, it will not be for his or her people. If the senior pastor hires a staff person to do the groups, then this ministry will be just another department like all the other good things the church offers—another choice among many, but not really as important in the life of a growing Christian as it was in Acts.

There are four major ways a senior pastor can stay in leadership of small groups:

1. Organize the total church so that everyone on staff supervises small groups—more than a department mentality.
2. Protect lay pastors and groups from the pressure of promoting church stuff instead of encouraging them to be a group of people in koinonia.
3. Preach about how God has called and gifted all believers for ministry, and then give them recognition with illustrations and testimonies. The preaching can be reinforced if the groups discuss the discussion questions the pastor has written.
4. Write the calendar to reflect the vision/passion for group life.

Small-Group Conviction Test

1. Speaking for myself, I am
   ___ fully convinced of the biblical priority for small groups.
   ___ mostly convinced of the biblical priority for small groups.
   ___ slightly convinced of the biblical priority for small groups.
   ___ not convinced there is a biblical priority for small groups.

2. For the most part, I think my church leadership is
   ___ fully convinced of the biblical priority for small groups.
   ___ mostly convinced of the biblical priority for small groups.
   ___ slightly convinced of the biblical priority for small groups.
   ___ not convinced there is a biblical priority for small groups.

3. For the most part, I think my senior pastor is
   ___ fully convinced of the biblical priority for small groups.
   ___ mostly convinced of the biblical priority for small groups.
   ___ slightly convinced of the biblical priority for small groups.
   ___ not convinced there is a biblical priority for small groups.

✿ 6

How to Get Started
with a Pilot Group

Over the years many churches have tried to transition from a traditional program of ministry to a network of small groups. Many have tried; some have been successful. What can be learned from both? What steps can assure a pastor and the leaders of a local church that their energies will have good results in both individual and church growth? The steps and principles I have outlined here will certainly increase the chances for a small-group system to be in the winners' circle.

Principles

Start-up Principle No. 1: *Have a head coach.* Every team needs a coach, and every staff of coaches needs a head coach. This fits with God's design for church life found in Eph. 4:11-13. The senior pastor needs to be the head coach and give leadership until everyone participating (or not participating) knows that small-group ministry is the pastor's heartbeat. Every "assistant coach" and every team player is an extension of his or her pastor. The fact is that small-group ministry will never be a priority commitment for the church if it is not a priority commitment of the pastor. More than his "endorsement" with nice words and "recognition time" on Sunday, it must be as important to the pastor as it was to the first-century Church: right up there with the large-group events (Acts 20:20).

Even though the senior pastor delegates major responsibilities to the "assistant coaches" (both volunteer and salaried), he or she cannot just turn the whole game plan over to them with a pat on the shoulder. No, there is the development of each one's specialty (neighborhood groups, children's and youth groups, men's and ladies' groups, specialty groups, etc.), but with central leadership so every group is on the same page of the game plan.

The head coach (pastor) orchestrates the total ministry with (Acts) 20/20 vision, guarding and directing the various ministries toward common goals. When victory is won—everybody celebrates, not just a few.

An effective coach will also do what he or she expects the players to do. That principle is far different from my experience in high school gymnastics. Our coach tried to coach with a book! In the two years I was on the team, I never once saw him on an apparatus to say, "Floyd, this is how to do it." It was only, "Look at this diagram and do what you see drawn and then do this next move." Jesus was effective in the training of the Twelve because they saw Him do it as well as talk about it.

Start-up Principle No. 2: *Make mistakes.* Mistakes are helpers, not hindrances. Pastors and churches should expect mistakes and thank the Lord for them. They help chart the course with necessary adjustments that will keep small groups on the road. The goal is always in sight: Get everyone we possibly can into a healthy small group. But the way to that goal is sometimes bumpy and filled with other surprises. When mistakes are made, quickly admit them, learn from them, restate the goal, and move ahead. Please don't let a mistake or two or even 50 cause you to turn back. Stand firm with a humble spirit, and God will give the increase.

Make sure you generate a reasonable number of mistakes. I know that comes naturally to some people, but too many executives are so afraid of error that they rigidify their organization with checks and counterchecks, discourage innovation, and, in the end, so structure themselves that they will miss the kind of offbeat opportunity that can send a company skyrocketing. So take a look at your record, and if you can come to the end of a year and see that you haven't made any mistakes, then I say, brother, you just haven't tried everything you should have tried.

It is a cliché to say that we learn by our mistakes, but I'll state the case more strongly than that: I'll say you can't learn without mistakes.[1]

Start-up Principle No. 3: Start small. It is the principle of the mustard seed. Plant it and care for it, and it will grow up naturally to be strong and a reproducing agent. The key is to plant the kind of group you want to be multiplied. Some pastors have made the mistake of planting "a class for leaders" and have been disappointed when they produced little classes instead of caring groups. Plan for the expanding multiplication of what you plant.

Most of the time a church has a desire to begin several groups at once, but that's not possible because of the lack of (or only a few) trained leaders. So they yield to the temptation of mass-producing leaders with a teacher-to-student dynamic in a church classroom. Pastors fall into this innocently, because that's how they were trained!

Just stop and realize what you want to grow: care groups in homes. OK—plant that kind of group. As an illustration, a pastor asked me once in a seminar how I would start groups in his church of 300 Sunday attenders. My answer would have been the same for a church of 1,000. I said I would start three pilot groups: an early-morning men's group that I would lead, a neighborhood ladies' group my wife would lead, and one mixed group we would lead together. "That's all?" he asked. I was trying to emphasize the importance of starting small and growing up leaders the same way Jesus and the apostles did it—on the job.

Steps

Step 1: Receive God's vision. There is no substitute for having a clear vision of what God wants in the church and the community. When you know you want what God wants, you have the assurance He will provide the resources necessary to bring it to pass.

Every church is unique in its gifting and in its personality. Every community is unique in its cultural ways of doing things. Ideas and resources are published and readily available, but each church and community will need God's vision that is uniquely theirs.

When seeking and receiving God's vision for a small-group ministry, keep two guidelines in place. First, make sure the vision is big enough to require God's help and power. Small ideas and small dreams give God's people nothing to pray about—nothing that requires faith to be exercised. Get God's vision, and prayer will be a way of life. Second, make sure the vision is big enough to bring out the best of you. Man-sized visions call only for average commitment and mediocre effort.

Step 2: Decide that a system of small groups is God's plan for the church. It is not another program option among many. It is not an idea that appears to be workable. It is not an experiment to "try out" on a group that has seen so many notebooks and tapes they are about to croak. No, a decision must be made first; then go after the planning of a strategy to see it completed. It is *make a decision and then solve the problems*. The decision is made before all the questions are answered and before some are even asked. Oh yes—this *is* God's plan for the church.

Step 3: Ask permission to lead. This is a crucial step. Many pastors have assumed they are leading a congregation because they have the title, but if they have no one following, they are only taking a walk. Notice this step is "Ask for permission to lead," not "Ask for permission for a program." We are not discussing an agenda item for a board meeting. The vision has been received (step 1), a decision has been made (step 2), and those two are communicated. The strategy is not yet confirmed, mistakes are yet to be made, but permission to lead must be given or a church will never experience God's design for churches to minister to each other's needs in small groups.

Step 4: Inventory the small groups you already have and determine the best way to meet the needs of the people in those groups. List all the small groups that meet regularly in the life of your church for whatever reason. Before starting a network of groups that are specifically designed to be circles of love, it is good to find ways to help existing groups become more caregiving in structure. They need to be more encouraging, more nurturing, listening more to each other, more forgiving, praying more for needs, and more edifying, along with their regular reasons for meeting.

It is not a loving thing just to chop off some things that seem to be "in the way" of the new direction you desire for the church. My advice is to start a small pilot group and help the existing groups be more healthy for the people who find them to be meaningful. The midweek service at the church is a good example. Instead of locking the door to those who do attend, leave it open and start a pilot group in someone's home. Avoid the guilt trips on people who choose to be in one and not the other.

Step 5: "Select" participants for a pilot group. Guidelines for this step include the following:

a. Choose some potential leaders, but do not ask for a leadership commitment from them. If they said yes to being a leader some day, they would be making a commitment to something they had not yet experienced. Only ask them to be an active participant in a new group. They will be able to commit to leading their own group when they have experienced one.

b. Choose pioneers. Every church has both pioneers and settlers, but settlers will never help you start small groups. It's not that they are not good people or are unspiritual; it's just that they see life through different eyes. A settler's primary concern is to take care of what he or she already has. But a pioneer's primary concern is to move ahead, taking risks, with eyes on the horizon.

c. Choose a host home away from church. My preference for a pilot group is the home of a new Christian, because he or she has the best contacts for prospects. The host or hostess is a vital part of the leadership team and will be a key to the success of the group.

Step 6: Make sure the pilot group is a prototype of what you want multiplied groups to be. What you want reproduced is what you plant. It is in the prototype group where the mistakes are corrected until you are ready for production. In every way you can, make the pilot group look and sound and move and feel like what you want all those groups to be a year, two years, five years from now—such as the following:

a. An open group instead of a closed one. This means you will not invite too many (maybe three to five), because you want them each to invite others. Even unchurched people are invited to the pilot group so your future leaders will learn how to bring them to Christ and develop spiritual maturity.

b. A group that is more like a family than a service or a class where one person does most of the talking while the others sit in rows. The leader is primarily a caregiver, facilitating discussion in a circle of love. The goal is to build a healing fellowship (James 5:16).

c. A group where leadership skills are learned by practice and example rather than by lecture. For example, it is better to give a few guidelines for conversational prayer and then pray than to have a 30-minute monologue about how you do it! The very best place to train group leaders is in a healthy group.

Step 7: Multiply. The elapsed time before a pilot group is ready to birth a new one or more will vary. There are basically three factors to be considered: *(a) The spiritual maturity of the group participants, (b) the leadership skills of the group participants,* and *(c) the vision they have for small-group ministries.* In some cases the pilot group is ready to multiply in four to six weeks, while for others it may be as much as six months.

After some "on-the-job training," you are ready for

multiplication. Either an apprentice leader takes over the leadership of the original group as the pastor/coach chooses another apprentice and begins to prospect a new group, or an apprentice leader teams up with his or her own apprentice to go out and prospect a new group. Many times, since potential leaders have been invited to the pilot group, two or three groups can be formed at once in new host homes. *Note:* Not only do good group leaders cause multiplication to take place, but after getting a group established, they will move toward initiating another group in order to avoid what I call "personality stagnation."

Step 8: Have a weekly group for leaders. The leaders of the growing network of groups need to be brought together regularly with their pastor/coach. By attending a weekly meeting, they will actually be saving themselves time—because this becomes their "preparation time." They will practice doing the same three things in this hour that they will do in their groups: share life, pray for each other, and discuss the same lesson outline they will be using. Notice this is a *group* for leaders, *not* a class. Although there will be skill training as you go along, it needs to be nurture-oriented. The leaders will then have a weekly model group to follow.

In the meeting the leaders will receive inspiration, motivation, new assignments, and a chance to report joys and challenges. They will also have opportunities to pray and to be prayed for. In a very real way, the pilot group becomes a permanent, ongoing group. It will very quickly become the highlight of the week for the "coach," who gets to do what God called him or her to do (equip) and also for the team members, who want to make their lives count through ongoing ministry. It keeps everyone current with the hows and whys of what they are doing.

And to the same degree your leaders are cared for, they will care for their people.

Notice the leaders' meeting is step 8, not even in the first three! To start a training hour for leaders without groups to lead would make the training sterile. In fact, it might even be dangerous to start training leaders who have no followers!

In conclusion, I am convinced that a pilot group is the best way to start any new ministry. Following the three principles and the eight steps will grow a network of groups inside any church, such as men's groups, ladies' groups, children's groups, singles' groups, 12-step recovery groups, and so on.

❀ 7

How to Grow Healthy
Small Groups

When developing a small-group ministry in a local church, it is important to *(a)* follow up on the vision God gives, *(b)* train the leaders God raises up, *(c)* organize a system that gives everyone an opportunity to meet with a "family," and *(d)* provide a lesson guide that will help them apply the Scripture to daily life. But, all that work is for *nothing* if good things do not happen when the people actually come together in their groups. If the dynamics that produce health and growth are not present in the group meeting, then all of the other things listed above cannot produce life.

What are those principles that have proven to be effective in successful groups? There are four that absolutely cannot be ignored if a group is to be healthy and growing. We've learned them the hard way—by not doing them! As a result of evaluating why a group has become sick or perhaps has even died, we have determined these four. Now your groups don't have to make the same mistakes.

Before explaining the four principles, let's take a quick look at the portrait of a healthy group. Notice the leadership team is in place, including someone to care for the children (if necessary) and a coach who visits occasionally. Notice also the variety of group members—each committed to individual and corporate nurture and growth.

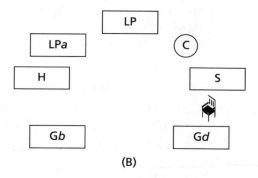

(B)

LP—Lay pastor. The leader of the group and many times a leader couple.

LPa—Lay pastor apprentice or assistant group leader. Perhaps an apprentice couple.

H—Host/Hostess. The person(s) responsible for making everybody comfortable and welcomed, both regular attenders and guests.

Gb—Grace builder. The person God brings to a group who continually tests the boundaries.

(B)—The person who has the responsibility to care for the children. Not every group will provide this for their people.

Gd—Growing disciple. The person who rarely ever misses a group meeting and is alive and excited about his or her faith.

—The empty chair that helps a group focus in prayer for the person who will accept an invitation and visit the group next week.

S—Seeker. The person who has not yet made a commitment to Christ but is searching for God's purpose in his or her life.

C—Coach. The person who visits the group occasionally to encourage the leadership team and fellowship with the people.

Principle 1: Balance

Most of the time when a group has made a good start but sickness and/or death has come, this number one principle has been neglected. There are three things that need to happen each time the group meets: the sharing of life, the praying for each other, and the application of the Bible to daily life. All three must be part of the group experience but must be kept in balance to assure the long-term health of the group. As a result of a balanced group, healthy and well-balanced disciples will be produced.

When a group becomes dominated with the sharing of life (as important as that is for groups), they are cheating themselves out of time for prayer and Bible application. People will not grow much in their faith if prayer and God's Word are minimized. In fact, we've discovered that people will not come back to groups that are sharing, sharing, sharing. No one wants to visit the city dump once each week! And most leaders don't know what to do with all the stuff people want to bring to a group. As vitally important as sharing is, it must be kept in balance.

When a group becomes primarily a prayer meeting, the result is the same. As important as intercessory prayer is to the life of a group, if prayer is allowed to dominate the time, then the group is off balance. The group has little time left for the sharing of life and discovering truth for daily life. There will be times, however, when a person arrives with an unusually heavy burden that must be shared and prayer given. In that one group meeting the most important thing is to lovingly care for that person. But for the long-term health of the group, balance is the goal.

When a group becomes mostly a Bible study, then again they are out of balance and only students will attend. It is easy for this kind of group to become a class, where a teacher gives a lesson, instead of a family, where everyone contributes. There will be times when a passage of Scripture really comes alive and an unusual amount of time is given to it. That's great! But be careful to get back in balance in the following weeks, or the group will cease to be healthy.

When referring to the balance principle, I am not suggesting three 20-minute segments in a one-hour meeting or three 30-minute segments in a 90-minute meeting. That would be balance, all right, but much too mechanical. Please refer to the suggested order of a group meeting below and the balancing of the parts of an effective group.

Suggested Order for a Successful Group Meeting
    Fellowship with Those Who Come Early
    Welcome Words
        Introduction of guests
        Get-acquainted activity
    Worship
        Thanksgiving prayer
        Singing *(optional)*
        Praise reports
        Expressions of appreciation for each other
    Intercessory Prayer

> A need expressed
> Several lead in prayer
> Thank You, Lord
> *(sequence repeated as time permits)*
> Discussion of Bible Lesson
>> Seek full participation
>> Seek practical application
> Closing Prayer
>> Personal commitment of the biblical
>> truth discussed
> Fellowship with Those Who Want to Stay

Instead of three equal segments, the three are mingled throughout the meeting: sharing, praying, sharing, discussing, praying, discussing, sharing, praying, and so on. It flows, but with balance. Now let's look at each part more closely.

Sharing of life. There is nothing in a group like a life-centered testimony to illustrate what is being taught. It causes the written Word to become the living Word. Trust is developed and maintained by the honest heart-to-heart sharing of the people in a group. And then, in that climate of trust, the Holy Spirit does His best work of illuminating the Scripture in a personal way.

Also, when a person shares with a group, he or she feels more a part of the group. If it is a joy or a sorrow, a success or a failure, something wonderful happens when his or her "family" loves a person enough to listen and encourage. Every one of us has at least one hurt and at least one dream, even if we have never shared them with another person. God seems very near when we share either or both.

We never outgrow our need to share our need, to ask for the help of other Christians. When a leader has a need, he or she should quickly ask his or her group for help. By the leader's being vulnerable, the group discovers that it is a safe place for them too. Of course, in all the sharing of a small group, we must guard the integrity of the group by keeping to ourselves the confidential things shared. We are family, and we trust and defend each other (see 1 Cor. 13:7, TLB).

Once in a while a person might want to "share" someone else's faults. At times these come in the clever disguise of a prayer request. When this happens, the leader must take leadership by reminding the group of James 5:16 and noting that it is not the purpose of the group to talk about other people's faults—only our own. The sharing in a group is personal, not a church-sponsored gossip session!

Conversational prayer. Praying out loud in a group makes many people nervous. They are afraid of sounding stupid or of not saying the "right" words. Practice of conversational prayer in a loving atmosphere provided by a small group will certainly help alleviate those fears.

Having a conversation together with God is a quick way to build unity in a group. Most of the time a group will have the opportunity to pray together three times in the course of a meeting: first by praising the Lord and acknowledging His presence, then by praying for each other, and in closing to pray about applying the truth that was discussed.

Most people who have learned to pray "traditional" prayers will have difficulty relearning how to pray conversationally. The popular myth about conversational prayer is that it is sentence prayers. No, it is simply praying like we talk, and we do not talk to each other in sentences. We talk in topics and use personal words like

"I," "me," and "my," instead of general words like "we," "us," and "our."

A request is made known, and everyone can say to the Lord anything he or she wants to say about that need before going on to the next request. The best way to "close" a topic is to pray such things as, "Thank You, Lord," and "We commit this, Lord, to Your care." Each person's prayer is brief and spontaneous so that everyone can pray and be prayed for.

Through the years I have discovered that the best teachers of conversational prayer are children. They have not learned to pray long and fancy prayers; they just pray with honest, personal words of faith, hope, and love.

Application of the Bible. This part of a healthy and growing group is kept in balance with the sharing and praying. However, our goal is more than gaining more Bible knowledge. Our goal is to allow the truth to make a difference in our daily lives. God has called us to be "doers of the word, and not hearers only" (James 1:22, KJV; see also Matt. 7:24-27).

Small-group discussion has application as its goal, without the group members doing homework and the study following an in-depth analytical format. The church needs to provide an educational ministry to meet those needs. Obviously we must have knowledge before it can be put into our lives, but applying the truth is our goal. Chapter 13, "How to Write Dialogue Questions," will illustrate how this is done.

To help us reach that goal, I recommend the use of a discussion guide along with our open Bibles. Not that other books are not helpful, but we want our people to interact with God's Word more than interacting with what another person says the Bible says. We believe the Bible is our only authority and contains everything necessary for our salvation and the Christian walk. The Holy Spirit is committed to respeak its truths so we can know what pleases the Lord (Eph. 5:10) and be successful in every area of our lives. With the Holy Spirit to guide us into all truth (John 14:26), with our Bibles opened before us, and surrounded by so much love from God's people, we have a life-changing combination every time we meet.

Principle 2: Participation

The next time you are about 20 minutes into a group meeting and all of a sudden you have that feeling surge through you, like, "This is really a great meeting—I'm glad I'm here!" just stop your mental tape and rewind it to find out what just happened to make you feel that way. You'll discover participation has reached a higher level. Either several people have responded to a discussion question, or someone has asked a question about the question, or someone who is normally very quiet has just expressed himself or herself, or an accompanying verse is shared with personal insight.

Even though participation is the key to the success of a group meeting, there will always be some challenges for us to reach that goal. For example, the seating arrangement will make a big difference in the way people participate. The best is a circle with only one empty chair (for the person who is expected to come next week). Everyone can see and be seen, hear and be heard. Chairs in a room need to be in a circle rather than a U-shape so the people on the ends do not feel isolated. When I have met men's groups in a restaurant and we have more than eight, the men at the ends have difficulty seeing, and it's hard for them to hear each other's prayers and comments.

Sometimes group leaders want participation so much that they pull little tricks out of their bag to get it—such as directly asking someone to pray, read, or speak who is too timid to do it on his or her own. This is a very awkward thing for that person. It also sets up a negative dynamic in the group. The group participants are left edgy because they're afraid they'll be called on next.

Another popular trick that causes tension in a group is taking turns around the circle to read verses of Scripture or to say sentence prayers about an announced topic. That gets 100% participation (maybe), but it's a little game that misses the ultimate goal of helping people want to offer their thoughts out loud.

Before looking at two challenges, there is one more note to help leaders reach the goal of total participation. The leader is to be the leader, not the final authority with the last word of every discussion. He or she is to be the facilitator or guide, making all persons feel comfortable enough to enter in at any time. And then when they do, a few simple little words like "Thank you, _____" and "_____; I appreciate your sharing that" will do wonderful things in freeing up group participation.

Two challenges of high participation. *Challenge No. 1: The person who talks too much.* Have you ever been in a small group with this person? I have. He or she takes a breath in the middle of a sentence so no one can interrupt at the end of the sentence. And then, when someone else *does* get to say something, the person finishes that individual's sentence, and away he or she goes. I guess this is a universal problem. If 10 people get together, some of them will talk too much and some hardly at all. It's OK to be shy and quiet, and it's OK to be outgoing and talkative. But in order to have a healthy and growing group, those who are on both ends of the spectrum need to move a little toward the center—and everyone in the group wins.

Through the years I have discovered that people who talk too much are lonely, and their talking is their reaching out for acceptance. But their method is actually having the opposite affect! If the person persists, perhaps a statement such as one of these would be helpful:

- Thank you for your comments. Now let's hear what someone else has to say.
- Let's continue now with our lesson.
- Let's hear from someone who hasn't had a chance yet to talk.

Eventually the individual will appreciate your loving way of helping him or her be quiet, because down inside his or her spirit the person doesn't want to be a "turn-off."

Challenge No. 2: The person who wants to argue. There are two things that will divide groups that otherwise love each other: doctrine and politics. Polarity of the group between "us" and "them" is guaranteed if the leader refuses to lead in reinforcing this principle of group life: we just cannot allow doctrinal discussion that is divisive or argumentative. Obviously, we cannot study the Bible without doctrine being a part of the discussion, but I am referring to the division that hurts instead of heals.

Many people would rather introduce controversy than give attention to what needs to happen in their own lives. Their discussion of some "pet doctrine" serves only as a smoke screen to hide their own real needs. An effective leader will stop this runaway train who wants to go down his or her own track. A loving statement such as this might be helpful: "It's not our purpose to discuss divisive doctrines here. If you have a question about that, give our pastor a call, and he'll [or she'll] help you with it. Let's go on now with our lesson." Very, very few people will ever call a pastor to discuss doctrinal differences. So that lets us know that the person's real motivation is to control the group. The leader just cannot allow that to happen by surrendering leadership to them.

Principle 3: Loving Response

To respond lovingly immediately to a need expressed is a skill best learned in a family—the original small group. Once it is learned, it affects all the other relationships of life (friends, work associates, ministry). After giving us the "love chapter" (1 Cor. 13), Paul encourages us to make this agape love our number one aim. And when does this love take action? It begins when we listen to people in the group and respond as soon as a need is expressed. Love does not respond later.

For clarification, let's apply this principle to the three parts of a healthy, growing group:

Sharing of life. How do you help a group of people learn to "be a family" and share God's love with each other? Probably the very best way is for the leader to set the example before them each week and between meetings. An effective leader is a loving caregiver, who opens areas of his or her own life with I-messages and asks for prayer. The pattern and the promise for this is in James 5:16.

- Confess our faults to each other.
- Pray for each other.
- Become a healing fellowship.

Every time we are together, we have opportunity to practice giving love's response by building each other up with words of affirmation, appreciation, and blessing (Heb. 10:25). We commit ourselves to each other to be everything we can be for God. We want to build (and in some cases rebuild) healthy self-esteem in each other (Rom. 14:19).

Conversational prayer. During the intercessory prayer time, the temptation will be to gather all the prayer requests and then enter into prayer. Please don't yield to that temptation. The most loving thing is to respond immediately to the request. There is something very unloving about letting a person hang when he or she has just shared a concern from his or her life. By the time a group has finished praying for each other's needs, they will have a prayer list to take home, but avoid starting with a list. Most of the time when a list is made first, the first person who prays mentions everything on the list and everybody else listens. That's great, but that's not conversational prayer!

Another way to respond lovingly in prayer is to place a chair in the middle of the circle. While a person sits in the "love seat," the others gather around and gently lay their hands on him or her. God answers prayers of faith and love. Be careful, though, when a person lets you pray for him or her this way that the group enters into prayer and not a chance to preach little bits of advice. Let love lead the way to Jesus. Let the praying be another example of "love in action."

Application of the Bible. Every person in the group is encouraged to share his or her own life as the Scripture passage is discussed. The questions from the lesson guide are written so we can share from our hearts and not just with our heads. Every person is made to feel that his or her questions and thoughts are important. Generous amounts of "Thank you," "That's a new insight," and "That's an interesting point" will help everyone feel like a member of the family. Even the person (the grace builder) who has just said something totally off track will be thankful for having a "family."

Remember: our goal is dialogue. Groups that have dialogue with lots of love will attract hurting and troubled people. Where else can they go but to the Lord to find peace, joy, stability, and healing in their lives?

However, the group is not a therapy session, and the leader is not an amateur psychologist. People with deep emotional problems must be referred to competent counsel. That would be love's response.

Principle 4: Follow-up

One of the most effective ways to keep groups healthy and the meetings alive is faithful and consistent follow-up. Regular attenders are called and given words of encouragement and prayer concern. Those who are absent are reminded of the group's love, but not in the form of a guilt trip that a delinquent member has to endure. New people are called in friendship and invited to visit. In fact, the follow-up of the people is the bigger part of a small-group ministry. The actual meeting together is just the excuse for getting to do this larger ministry.

This one-to-one caregiving, away from the group, is something everyone gets to do, but especially the leadership team. Shepherding. Pastoring. Parenting. It means using the telephone as an instrument of ministry. It's true: the phone many times is an interrupter, an intruder. But we should be praising the Lord for the telephone, because it helps us do our ministry.

When using the telephone in ministry, here are three helpful guidelines.

   a. Pray for yourself before dialing the number, that God would make you an instrument of love, that

He would cleanse your spirit and give you wisdom.

b. Pray with the person if that is appropriate. It is that connecting that helps him or her know God is near and not long-distance.

c. Pray after the contact, that God will continue to anoint and bless. Be available to serve in Jesus' name in the future.

Another part of follow-up is the tender loving care that a grace builder needs. It is possible that a troubled person can be so disruptive in a group that people no longer want to attend. Even though we encourage lots of sharing in the group, we cannot surrender leadership to a troubled person. If a person is allowed continually to demand the group's attention, it may be a fatal blow to the health of that group. It has happened many times to other groups, so we can learn from them.

So what can be done? Talk with the person away from the group and explain *what* the problem is and not *who* the problem is. That would only make the person defensive and cause the problem instead of the solution to grow. Also, if a leader needs help with a grace builder, the pastor stands ready to assist. He has probably had some experiences with people like this before!

An indispensable tool for effective follow-up is a current responsibility list. The list is compiled by the leadership team, but everyone in the group gets to help with it in two ways:

1. They help by prospecting new people—because the best source is the people already in the group. To help keep the vision of outreach alive, pray for the person who will come next week to sit in the empty chair. Pray for that person and then go after him or her. New people brought into a group will keep the group alive

and healthy. New people will help a group become a "family of God" instead of a "holy club." Comfortable with each other? Yes. Exclusive? No.

2. By having an up-to-date responsibility list in everyone's hands, the group becomes *ours,* not just the leader's. Occasionally a special feature is planned (a special guest, a video, a dinner, a picnic), and everybody on the entire list is called. Names are assigned, and the invitations go out. If their names are not on a list, some of those people will be forgotten.

RESPONSIBILITY LIST

Meeting Place _____

Day and Time _____

NAME	CODE	PHONE NUMBER	REMARKS

CODES: Leader—L   Apprentice Leader—AL
Host/Hostess—H   Regular Attender—RA
Prospect—P   Occasional Attender—OA

Children and Small Groups

Question: What about the children? Good question! Do they meet with the adults in their small groups, or do they have separate meetings?

Answer: Every group is going to have to decide what is best for them. Listed below are some options that leaders can use to help their group decide what to do.[1]

1. The children are with the adults. Gasp! Most of us could very quickly list five good reasons why we should *not* include children in our group. But at least let's look at some reasons to have the children with us.

a. The parents have an excellent opportunity to have help as they build convictions and values in their children. This is especially attractive to single parents.

b. Children learn how to pray, celebrate, and edify in an extended family.

c. Adults learn to come to God with simplicity, awesome wonder, and great faith.[1]

d. New Christians are made to feel right at home because they can share and pray along with the children, who skip all the sophisticated stuff.

Be sure to plan the meeting to include some activities if children are present: singing action choruses, doing a skit, having a show-and-tell, coloring a picture, memorizing a verse, and so on. Discussing one Bible verse for 30 minutes is possible for some adults, but not for children.

2. The children have their own group, meeting at the same time as the adults in another part of the house or at a neighbor's home. A leader helps them accomplish the same three things the adults are doing in their group: sharing life with each other, learning how to pray for each other, and applying the Bible to their daily choices. The children will look forward to *their* group as much as the adults do to theirs. If a group chooses this option, the leader can be someone who has special gifting to do children's ministry, or the adults in the group can rotate as the leader of the children's group.

3. Have a half-and-half arrangement. The children meet with the adults for the early part of the meeting and then go to their own group while the adults discuss their lesson. The children will either do a lesson/activity of their own or receive child care.

4. Hire someone to do child care. This can be in another part of the house or close by. If this option is chosen, everyone in the group contributes to the cost, not just the adults who brought children.

5. A church activity for children. Some churches are localized in such a way that they can schedule most of their small groups on the same evening, and the parents can drop off their children at the church for an enriching experience planned especially for them. Caution! This plan needs to include a small-group experience for the leaders who care for the children so they don't miss out on the good things God gives to those who participate in a neighborhood group. Perhaps the leaders' planning meeting could include some nurturing activities to meet the needs of the ministers to children.

6. Inform the people as they are invited to the group that no child care is provided. They will need to make their own arrangements.

Before concluding this section, I need to give a praise report about the first small group to impact my life other than my family. It was an after-school Bible club. I can remember running down Sixth Street one afternoon each week to the house of a lady who had special things planned for us. I learned so much, and it was fun! Somehow it was different in her home than it was in Sunday School. Looking back and also by observing what is being provided by some churches today, many reasons can be listed to have neighborhood small groups for children:

- Children growing up together in a neighborhood can be brought together on a spiritual level.
- They can develop habit patterns of caring for one another.
- When they are regularly praying for each other, they are going to care on a deeper level.
- They will learn to trust each other more.
- They will verbalize those "deeper things of life" that are usually held inside when they are surrounded by adults.
- They will develop deeper lifetime friendships.
- They will have the opportunity to live out the Word of God more openly.
- They will help each other "keep on track" with positive peer pressure.
- They will feel more secure in a support system as they grow into young adults.
- They will learn to take responsibility and develop leadership skills at an early age.

❊ 8

How to Develop the Leaders of Small Groups

The challenge of Rev. 3:20 is given to God's people and not to unbelievers, as it is commonly thought. God continues knocking and calling loud enough for a willing soul to hear. And what is the invitation? Open the door and let's have fellowship! And the fellowship with our Lord is so precious that we are tempted to stay and enjoy His presence. But, no, as important as the worship experience is for us, we are most like Jesus when we are serving.

The apostle Paul wrote to the Corinthians in the second letter (5:18-19) that God has committed to us the message of reconciliation. What an awesome responsibility! But who is the "us"? Answer: the reconciled ones. That's all of us, not just a few. Question: Are God's people the helpers, or are they ministers? Answer: God's people are ministers, but in many churches they are not given opportunity to minister. We need to develop a higher view of spiritual gifting and ministry of the believers than a church filled with helpers.

My all-time favorite story from the life and ministry of Jesus, when I was a child, was about His feeding of that great crowd of people from one boy's lunch. Recent-

114

ly I realized my childhood picture of what happened there that afternoon was mistaken. I thought Jesus took the boy's lunch that was brought to Him, thanked His Father for it, and broke it in such a way that this huge mound of food appeared, which had to be distributed. Wrong.

While reading Mark's account, in chapter 6, I discovered the miracle happened between verses 41 and 42. He received the lunch, thanked His Father for it, broke it, and gave it to His disciples. It was when they gave it away that it multiplied! And our Lord is still doing that today—He trusts us with *His* ministry. When we go out to give what we have received, miracles happen in our hands. John 14:12 is still true.

God works through people. He always has, and He always will. Not notebooks and tapes, not well-machined organizations, not just a few professionally trained persons—God works through ordinary people who are committed to love the people around them God's way.

Our primary objective in small-group ministry is not to build groups. Does that sound like a contradiction? We develop small groups so we can build leaders, because leaders build groups. It's as simple as that.

Recruiting New Leaders

Who is recruited and who does the recruiting? By far, the best recruiters are the small-group leaders we already have. They are growing in their own faith, and their witness is fresh and alive and enthusiastic. They have weekly contact with their people, helping them discover and develop their spiritual gifts. They have visions about their ministry growing beyond themselves as multiplication occurs. They are overtly leading a small group, but covertly they are training future leaders. They are seeking out new people to take their places.

One of the poorest recruiters in the church is the pastor. Not too many can identify with his or her Bible knowledge and theological training. The pastor may be a persuasive person, but is the commitment he or she gets from people directed to himself or herself or to the ministry? Sermons and publications will help, but the best recruiting will always be done in a small group and one to one.

The Cycle of Success (below) was given to me one day as I had lunch with my wife at a restaurant. The Lord gave it to me as I scribbled on a napkin. Perhaps it will help to illustrate where we find new leaders.

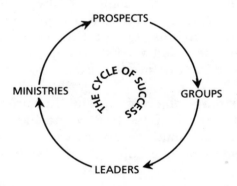

Here's how it works:

1. Recruit everyone possible as a prospect for a group—any kind of a group.
2. When they have become active in a group, they will grow and take more and more responsibility until they realize, "Oh, I think I could do this!"
3. The key to growth is *leaders*—God works through people. As soon as a person from a group comes to a training event, he or she is al-

pioneer vs. settler

ready half-trained because of the group life he or she has experienced.

4. With a new leader we are able to expand ministries, which immediately puts us in contact with more people who (1) need to be invited to a group and (2) raised up in that group until (3) they are ready to take leadership responsibility and (4) multiply ministry to more people (1)—and so on.

It appears the lack of committed laborers is not a new phenomenon. Even Jesus said the harvest was ready but to pray for more to go into the harvest (Luke 10:2).

Twice now I have been in a conference with Pastor Paul Yonggi Cho from Seoul, South Korea, when someone asked him where he gets all the leaders for his more than 60,000 cell groups. He smiles and answers, "New Christians." The pastors in the room all gasp, because they hold new Christians off for a while before letting them do meaningful ministry. Every new Christian has at least 20 non-Christians he or she is very close to. What a shame to miss the chance to bring them in because we felt it was too soon! How long did it take the Samaritan lady Jesus talked to at the well to get into ministry? Answer: *Long enough to go into the village and come back!*

Repeatedly through the years I have supervised groups in which I have seen the winning combination when new Christians and pioneer (not settler) Christians are teamed together. They encourage each other in unmistakable ways. The new Christian needs the wisdom of the pioneer; the pioneer needs the excitement of the new Christian. One has questions; the other has answers. It's the same winning method of Alcoholics Anonymous. The one who is just gaining sobriety is encouraged by the story of the one who has been sober for a

~~while—and knows he or she can make it too~~. The one who has been sober for a while is encouraged to see that the 12 steps still work.

While recruiting, we must understand that God has given *every* believer a call to ministry. This is a fourfold call that is upon us all. Not everyone is going to be a small-group leader, but every believer must answer to these four callings.

1. Missionary—Matt. 28:18-20. Notice that this is not a call reserved for a select few. Notice also that it has no age limits, no academic requirements, and no geographic restrictions. Just go, make disciples, baptize, and teach to obey. The challenge to *go* is the starting point. Go where? Outside our comfort zone! To do what? Share the good news of Jesus and stay with them until they are able to do the same for someone else.

2. Ambassador—2 Cor. 6:19-20. This is a high calling—to be the personal representative of the Almighty God. We recognize our citizenship is in a new nation (1 Pet. 2:9), and we are God's contact here on earth. We are not called to live a perfect life, but we are called to live a holy life as His ambassadors.

3. Shepherd—John 21:15-17. To be a shepherd is a call to sacrifice what might be convenient for ourselves for the benefit of our sheep. Three kinds of sheep may not make it without the help of a shepherd: those who have wandered away, those who have been led astray, and those who are down—too weak to come back to Father God without the loving care of a shepherd.

4. Servant—Matt. 20:28 and Rom. 12:11. I am convinced this is God's highest call—*to serve*. It's possible to become very pious and spiritual about serving God, but in John's first Epistle he makes it very clear that we serve God by serving people. Serving is very

ATF

practical and not always noticed and/or appreciated. However, as we continue to say, "Yes, Lord," He will bless us with creative opportunities to serve others. We are most like Jesus when we are serving.

Beyond the general fourfold call of all believers, we are always on the watch for "FAT" Christians (**F**aithful, **A**vailable, and **T**eachable). I have found that all three of those qualities are necessary for effective leadership in small-group ministry. Those who are available and teachable but do not follow through with responsibilities they accept cannot be leaders. If they are faithful and teachable but are too encumbered with other things, they have nothing left for ministry. If they are faithful and available but do not have a cooperative spirit (always wanting to do their own thing), they cannot be effective leaders. We rejoice whenever we find a "FAT" Christian and do our best to recruit him or her.

A great biblical illustration of the recruiting for ministry is found in Acts 6 and 7. Here was a man who was already ready to serve. Stephen was full of the Holy Spirit, full of wisdom, full of faith, full of grace, and full of power. But when was he discovered? When there was a need expressed in the church! The call went out about a growth problem, and Stephen stepped forward. How will our people realize their God-given potential? Answer: Call the best out of them; God has already put it there. Recruiting them is a process of helping people follow the steps of Heb. 11:1-3 with a clear vision of their ministry: see it, pray it, say it, do it.

Training New Leaders

On-the-job training is best. Elijah did it that way (2 Kings 2). Jesus did it that way. The apostles did it that way. Even today, Bible colleges and seminaries continue to hear from their graduates that the highlight of their training was the internship and/or field service.

The most common objective to a weekly training meeting is lack of time. To answer that, we ask for a minimum of only three hours: one for training, one for the group meeting, and one for follow-up care of their people. We call our leaders' meeting a "huddle" because we want to emphasize the team effort. By coming together with the coach, we can stay on the same page of the game plan and learn from each other as we go. As soon as a small-group leader has a potential leader coming up in the group, that individual can be invited to come along to the huddle. This person discovers the meeting is not a class (it is a model group) and can begin to take more responsibility in the group and sign up for the next formal training event (described in chapter 12).

Several years ago two pastors were in my office to talk about small-group ministries. They were very concerned about how much training these leaders had received. I told them they had completed a weekend of training. And when they asked (with emphasis), "That's it?" I told them that they also came to weekly training as long as they wanted to be in leadership. When they asked what kind of training happened there, I explained it somewhat in the three parts listed below. One of them wrinkled up his face and asked, "You *have* to go to that every week?" Obviously, he was thinking with a mind-set that this was a leaders' class. No, not at all. This is a *huddle*. Remember, as a pastor I serve as a coach, and these leaders form my team. My success is in their success—so my meeting with them and my leaders with me is a highlight of our week. This hour together is not for a class; it is a group experience.

There are three purposes served in the weekly training.

1. Inspiration. Praise reports are given from the leaders, and everyone is encouraged. Problems are discussed and prayers of fellow leaders have a lifting effect on everyone. Reports by the pastor about God's moving in the total life of the church adds to the momentum. We want our leaders for the long term and know that's not possible without morale.

2. Information. Coming together once each week actually is a time-saver for the leaders. Their preparation time is almost nothing. After training, they can go right out and lead a group without doing any homework. They also have a chance to bring a written report about their previous week's ministry to training and receive assignments for the new week. Various ministry skills are sharpened from time to time.

3. Illustration. As much as possible, the weekly training is a model group—doing the same three things a group does together: sharing, praying, discussing. The sharing is about personal things and ministry joys and struggles. The praying is worship, intercession, and commitment. The discussion is with the same guide the leaders will use in their groups. It is as much on-the-job training as we can do. It also gives the pastor some top-quality time with his "front-line troops." He hears them report about successes and failures. They hear him report successes and failure. They are reminded that their ministry is an important part of the total life of the church. The pastor is reminded of the pastoral care that goes on each week. The pastor and the leaders are glad to be in the huddle.

Motivating Leaders

Axiom: People volunteer for lofty reasons and quit for mundane reasons.

Since we are not paying our people to lead small groups and to do the pastoral care of their people, we do not have the opportunity to give them a raise for a job well done or fire them when they goof up. How, then, do we motivate them in this ministry?

1. Depend on the Holy Spirit to be active in their lives, and commit them to Him in daily prayer.

2. Communicate the vision and the strategy of small groups every opportunity we have. Use word pictures to dramatize the need.

3. Create a climate of love. Fear and guilt are effective motivators, but only for the short term.

4. Answer their ongoing questions about "What's in it for me?" Remind them how they help themselves when they help others. Remind them their work has eternal value.

5. Give public recognition for faithful ministry.

6. Share ministry information with the "team" that is not given to the whole congregation. They will realize they are on the inside of what's happening in the church.

7. Give them permission to say a positive no to other things so they can keep their singleness of purpose.

Supervising Small-Group Leaders

In order for a bird to fly, it needs to have two wings. That's also true for a small-group ministry, and the two wings are *permission* and *supervision*. If either one gets too strong (or too weak), the ministry cannot fly. For example, if a church teaches that all believers have a call to ministry and sends them out with lots of freedom but little if any "coming alongside them" with accountability, the believers will only go in circles. Also, if the policies and procedures and reports and meetings are so heavy, with a minimum of releasing for ministry, they are flying in circles again!

The systematic supervision of all our small groups is very important in the development of leaders and in the ongoing growth of our groups. By setting appointments and visiting the groups, we can meet their new people and watch potential leaders in action. It also gives us a chance to assist with goal-setting and perhaps making suggestions about how to work with a "grace builder" who may be disrupting the group.

When a pastor or a coach or a captain visits a group to encourage them, the following objectives can be checked.

☐ The leadership team is in place (leader, apprentice, host/hostess).

☐ The responsibility list is up-to-date.

☐ Potential leaders are named.

☐ Observe the principles that keep groups healthy:
Balance
Participation
Loving response
Follow-up

Spiritual Growth of Leaders

The thrill of seeing groups give birth to new groups is wonderful. The celebration when another person is brought into the family of God is beyond words. But what about seeing the Holy Spirit give courage to a person who answers His call and grows at a fast rate by helping others grow? To be their "pastor-coach" is an awesome privilege. Following are some reports I have saved from a few of the hundreds I have received. These are only excerpts, but I'm sure the heartbeat can be felt in each one.

It is so rewarding to be a lay pastor. My friends told me how I've changed over the months, how I take the time to listen, and how I talk about Jesus. It just comes natural to me now; it's a part of my life. I thank Jesus for the new life He has given me.

* * *

I called the lady you gave me from a friendship card. She was so glad I'd called and enjoys how the people from our church take the time to follow up with love and prayers.

* * *

There were only the three of us for our group, and I said there must be a reason for this. Minutes later the phone rang, and an old friend was in the hospital to have open-heart surgery the next morning. We promptly went to the hospital. The lady rededicated her life, and we prayed for her healing. Her husband was also in the veterans' hospital. While she was in the recovery room Saturday night, he died. The family called us to come and minister to them and to their mother. We were present on Monday also when she was told of the event, and we prayed with her.

* * *

Yesterday was exciting. I felt unspeakable joy in the morning without knowing what was ahead. I left at noon to go to one of the old bars I used to go to, to leave a tract in the rest room. I decided to stop and have a frozen yogurt instead. One of the owners, Margaret, was alone. I do not know why, but I began to tell her of my experience with Jesus. She began to tell me that even though she is always smiling for the customers, she is lonely, depressed, and had tried to commit suicide. She was so excited to learn that Jesus is still alive and not just a story. We sat down. I gave her *The Four Spiritual Laws* and my card in case she ever needed someone. I felt then I should ask her if she would like to receive Jesus Christ now. She nodded yes, so I took her hand, we bowed our heads, and prayed the sinner's prayer. Oh, praise the Lord! I'll take this any day instead of a bottle of Jim Beam!

* * *

A new guest in our group told me that she was not a born-again Christian. After explaining Rom. 10:9, she asked to be led in prayer to Jesus. Then something else happened. Two other people in our group said that they did not understand or know if they were *truly* born again either.

Because of the miracle of rebirth I have rated the quality of the group experience this week as a 10.

❦ 9

How to Lead a Group Instead of Teaching a Class

Since this happens to be one of the most challenging areas of developing a small-group ministry in a local church, we need to give it special attention. Over the years it seems that we have decided the best way to "do church" is to preach and teach. And so we schedule services and classes until the day we meet in a small group. The temptation then is to fall back on well-established patterns and do a little church service or a warmed-over Sunday School class in someone's home.

Group life is unique in the life of a growing Christian. And groups are different from classes in many ways. Following are a few of those differences.

Leadership Is a Team Effort

Leadership of a group happens best when a team leads instead of just one person trying to do it all. God gives ministry abilities to people in a variety of ways. No one is complete in himself or herself. It's kind of like God's design for a family, having both a mom and a dad, each with his or her own strengths. They're different, but they complement each other. They're like a well-coached athletic team or a well-orchestrated music ensemble.

As leaders, all of us get sidetracked and/or down occasionally. If we are alone when that happens, our group is in real trouble (Eccles. 4:9-12). We need a team in place to give support and encouragement. Let's remember that we're in this for the long term and to avoid "burnout" of leaders. We work as a team.

The spiritual gifts a person has will help determine his or her part in the leadership of a group. With this in mind, the responsibilities will probably still be somewhat like this:

Group Leader or Couple—Guide the group through the three parts of an effective meeting, raise up an apprentice leader, bring a report to the pastor/coach.

Apprentice Leader or Couple—Practice doing the same things the leader does during the meeting and nurturing the people between meetings.

Host and/or Hostess—Have a genuine interest in each person who comes and make him or her comfortable, arrange the chairs to assist the participation dynamic in the group, plan the refreshment schedule to include everyone.

The shared responsibility of leading a group also will help develop new leaders. This is essential as we continue multiplying God's grace through groups. Where else are we going to find and train leaders?

Leaders Are Lay Pastors

More than teachers, more than group leaders—these special people who lead our groups are pastors in every sense of that word. Listed below are some of the things successful leaders will be doing to help them pastor their people.

1. Leaders follow. It is Christ who leads us. Our part is to follow our Lord with a "Yes, Lord" attitude. Following the Lord with a submissive attitude is truly an adventure. The weeks, months, and years unfold with a variety of opportunities to bless the lives of the people we serve. But it's all such a human effort without the Lordship of Jesus and the counsel of the Holy Spirit in our lives. It is our following that qualifies us to lead. To the same degree we are following, we are effective in leading.

2. Leaders stay spiritually tuned up. They do whatever it takes. The Holy Spirit will be hindered if we as leaders are spiritually indifferent or troubled with our own unconfessed sins. If we are not free to the working of the Holy Spirit in our own lives, we can hardly be channels for His working in the group. Whatever it costs, let's make the commitment to be tuned instruments of God's love.

3. Leaders lead in love. Lovingly caring for those in our small group is not something we do just for them; it is a way of life. Love, acceptance, and forgiveness are given to everyone around us. Our greatest need is to love and be loved. Some people are easier to love than others. Have you noticed? There are those who are so easy to be with; their attitudes are so positive, and they always seem to bless us with encouraging words. And then there are a few "grace builders" in each of our lives. Do they need love? Yes, they do—even if our love to them is not returned! As a child of God whose life has been blessed, we choose to bless, to heal, to lift, to love in Jesus' name.

4. Leaders are *learning* leaders. We don't even try to have all the answers. We do not expect our leaders to know all the answers before they lead a group. We wouldn't have many leaders, would we? The best leaders are good learners. It's OK to say often, "I don't know."

Also, when a leader doesn't have a quick answer (or even when he or she does) it's a good plan to say simply, "Does someone have an answer for us?"

5. Leaders hang loose. A relaxed spirit in the group will create a climate in which sharing, praying, and discussion will grow rapidly. This quality in a leader can be developed with guidelines, such as the following:

　a. We seek an honesty and openness that is not afraid to discuss or consider other points of view. Trust the Holy Spirit to be our Teacher.

　b. It is a tremendous asset when leaders accept themselves as persons of worth and can then reach out to others and make them comfortable with who they are.

　c. Good leaders learn to be shockproof, not judgmental or harsh or overly opinionated—not overly reactive when an individual says something that "goes against the grain."

　d. If we create a loving atmosphere, *the Holy Spirit will do His work.* That's a promise!

6. Leaders laugh a lot. A good sense of humor is a valuable asset for leaders. We don't take ourselves too seriously. This does not mean that leaders are good joke tellers, but they have a healthy and attractive view of life, a freedom in their spirits that allows laughter to flow. According to Prov. 17:22, laughter does wonderful things for us![1]

Relationships over Content

Building relationships is important for people in a class, but it is not a *primary* concern. Building relationships *is* a primary concern in a group, though. The content-oriented groups in a local church should be part of the education ministry. There are many ways bonding can happen in the life of a small group, but it happens best when we listen.

Several years ago I found the following verse. It influenced me then, and it still does. I trust it will help others to become more effective listeners for the benefit of those we love.

LISTEN

When I ask you
To listen
And you start
Giving advice,
You have not done what I asked.

When I ask you
To listen
And you begin
To tell me why I shouldn't feel the way I do,
You are trampling on my feelings.

When I ask you
To listen
And you feel
You have to do something to solve my problem,
You have failed me,
Strange as that may seem.

Listen.
All I asked you to do
Was listen,
Not talk,
Or do—
Just hear
Me.

I can do for myself;
I'm not helpless . . .
Perhaps discouraged or faltering,
But not helpless.

When you do something
For me
That I need to do for myself,
You contribute to my fear and weakness.

But,
When you accept as a fact
That I feel what I feel,
No matter how irrational,
Then I can stop trying to convince you
And get on with understanding
What's behind that irrational feeling.

And,
When that's clear,
The answers will be obvious,
And I won't need any
Advice.[2]

—Author unknown

In order to "break the ice" and help sharing of personal thoughts flow, leaders will occasionally want to ask some nonthreatening questions. They are nonthreatening because every answer is the right answer. Everyone has the opportunity to listen, and by listening become better acquainted with the other persons. Perhaps only one question is tossed out and everyone who wants to can respond. Or, to give more variety, the questions (such as those listed below) may be written on pieces of paper to be drawn out of a basket.

Take advantage of the sharing time to affirm each other.

Questions Dealing with the Past

1. Tell about the neatest birthday present you ever received.
2. Share one of the happiest days of your life.
3. What is the best advice you ever received?
4. What can you identify as a "turning point" in your life?
5. Share a time when your feelings were hurt.
6. Share a time when you believe you were led by God.
7. If you had the power to re-create yourself, what are two things you would not change?
8. Name one book (other than the Bible) that has had significant influence on your life. Why?

Questions Dealing with the Present

1. How do you tune into God?
2. How would you describe yourself to someone who does not know you?
3. Describe a typical day of your life.
4. If you had to move and could take only three things with you, what would you take?
5. Give three words to describe how you feel right now.
6. Name one model marriage. What is it you most admire about that marriage?
7. What, if anything, appeals to you about being rich?
8. If you were a mouse, what would be the most daring thing you would try to do while the cat was away?

Questions Dealing with the Future

1. Describe your ideal house and how you would furnish it.
2. What would you do if someone willed you a million dollars?
3. What is something you think God wants you to do?
4. What spiritual goal are you reaching for? Why?
5. If you could do anything you want this time next year, what would it be?
6. What epitaph do you want on your tombstone?
7. If for some reason you were forced to leave your home country, where would you go?
8. What do you most look forward to about growing old?
9. Name three people you would like to have praying for you in a difficult time.

Worship in a Group

Our worship time helps us concentrate when we come together from the busyness of life, from the responsibilities of the day. Worship helps us put the cares of life "outside" and sit at the feet of our Lord as Mary did (Luke 10:39). Our goal in worship is to bring every person into the very presence of our living Lord. Even though the worship time in a group is important, we must be careful not to let it become a miniservice.

By carefully planning a time of praise and worship involving singing, prayer, and sharing, we all become changed into the likeness of Jesus Christ, the One we adore, through our worship. Here are some suggestions:

1. Start small. Ask if anyone plays an instrument to accompany the singing (guitar, keyboard—or cassette tape).

2. Select two or three familiar choruses and learn a new one occasionally. Remember: we worship with untrained voices as well as the few trained ones.

3. Allow time for the Holy Spirit to minister. Avoid rushing through quiet times between songs, testimonies, and thanksgiving prayers.

4. Even though the worship time is planned beforehand, **let the Holy Spirit interrupt the plan** and give freedom and spontaneity.

The Relational Flow

Probably the most obvious difference between a class and a group is the amount of time given to the sharing of life. Interruptions are welcome! Not so in a class, because we need to get through the lesson. In a small group we can stop right in the midst of a lively discussion and pray with a person. We can stop right in the midst of a prayer and give a hug. We can say "I love you" and "I appreciate you" anytime. We think those wonderful things about each other all the time, but the small group gives us the opportunity to say them out loud. When that happens, both the blesser and the blessee are blessed.

One of my favorite cartoons of all time is the one in which a poor fellow is being told what a disgrace and loser he is. He is asked for his excuse for being such a failure. His answer: "I'm saving my good stuff!" And I've wanted to ask him, "For what?" Let's get real with each other and not hold back those words and actions that will bless someone. We have all been on the receiving end of that kind of spiritual anointing that came from one of God's instruments of love. Now let's pour it out over someone else's head like healing oil.

The Telephone as a Ministry Tool

One of the advantages a local church has when they have developed a network of small groups is the increase in pastoral care that is given. Meeting needs is a lot of guesswork if people who attend the worship services are not given the opportunity to communicate.

The response card is so much more than a record of their attendance. It is our link to the people in our lives in order to serve them. This "friendship card" is received with the tithes and offerings. Information that the church office might need is recorded and is then assigned to those who "pastor" the small groups. Those who are first-time visitors will receive a phone call, welcoming them to our church, and an invitation to visit their small group.

Below is a sample phone conversation. Also, those who have given us a prayer request will receive a call with lots of love, but not advice and prying questions. The goal is to pray with the person on the phone if that is desired, but if not, we simply remind them of our love and continued prayer. A phone conversation with a person who has turned in a prayer request card might also include an invitation to their small group.

Sample Phone Conversation with a First-time Visitor

Hello.

This is *(your name)*. Is *(visitor's name)* there, please? Thank you.

(When prospect is on the phone)

My name is *(your name)*. I'm a lay pastor at *(name of church)*, and I want you to know how pleased we were to have you attend our church. Is this a convenient time to talk?

What brought you to our church?

What did you enjoy most in the worship service?

Do you have any questions I could help you with?

One of the most exciting things I have experienced is a small-group fellowship and Bible study that meets at *(time)* on *(day)* evening.

The place where the group meets is not far from you, just *(general location of meeting place)*.

Do you think you might be able to come next *(day)* at *(time)*? That would be great.

I've enjoyed visiting with you, *(visitor's name)*.

The following is optional:

I'd like to meet you sometime. Maybe we could meet before or after church or Sunday School. Will you be in church this Sunday?

Great! How about meeting me over by the *(place)* at about *(time)*?

I'll probably be wearing a _____.

I'm looking forward to meeting you. Good-bye.

Note: Keep the conversation brief and friendly.

Sample Phone Conversation for a Prayer Request Follow-up

Hello.

This is *(your name)*.

Is *(person's name)* there, please? Thank you.

My name is *(your name)*, and I'm a lay pastor at the *(name of church)*. I was given the card you filled out last Sunday, and I wanted you to know I've been praying for *(request)*, which you mentioned on the back of the card.

How are things going? Seen any improvement yet? How can I pray for *(request)*? Well, I know God answers prayer.

Would it be all right if we had a prayer together right now for *(request)*?

Let's pray—

Sample prayer: Heavenly Father, thank You for Your love today. Thank You for Your power to do all things—nothing is impossible with You.

In full assurance of faith, we put *(name)* into Your loving hands. We ask for *(request),* and we expect good things to happen.

Lord, thank You for hearing us, and we give You praise.

In Jesus' name. Amen.

Thank you for letting me talk to you about this. I'll keep praying for *(name).* Would it be OK if I called you back sometime to see how you're getting along?

Good-bye.

❄ 10

How to Birth New Groups

Involving people in small groups is God's design for church life. As they continue to grow in their faith, they are going to need some ways to express what they have learned. Without vision and some opportunities for meaningful outreach, the groups will become stagnant and be nothing more than a "holy club." The group members who spend their primary energy on themselves will eventually fossilize.[1]

In John's Gospel (15:1-17), Jesus explained that the purpose of the vine (himself) and the branches (us) was to bear fruit. Looking good was not the goal. Being well organized was not the goal. The sap that nourished the vine and branches was not to be wasted on fruitless branches. They were to be cut off. And those who did have fruit were pruned so they could bear even more.[2] The size of a group does not determine its ability to reproduce. The fruit is determined by the health of the group.

Have you noticed there has been no mention of dividing or splitting groups to get new ones? Growth happens by multiplication, not division. A body grows by the multiplication of cells, not by making them larger.

Multiplication

For years I have been challenged with Paul's words

to Timothy about multiplication (2 Tim. 2:2). When I read those words, I see four chain links.

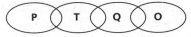

Paul said to teach selected people (Q)
what he (P) had taught him (T)
so they (Q) could teach others (O).

The challenge for me is not teaching what I have been taught. That's easy. The challenge is to teach in such a way that the learners can teach others. In fact, in my own family I am finding out what I gave to my children—by watching how they care for *their* children. And in total humility, I am a proud grandpa!

In order to multiply, three requirements must be followed, in the context of a relay race: (1) Several passes of the baton must be made. (2) Those who have the baton must pass it on. (3) The baton must be passed to the right people.

As in the challenge to Timothy, we have to be selective when we train leaders. Not every believer is a multiplier, and the selection has nothing to do with spirituality or favoritism. It has everything to do with vision and the person's willingness to do what God shows him or her. The decision that church leaders need to make is this: Am I going to do ministry or reproduce it?

The following true story from China is a dramatic example of what can happen when a congregation is operating with mission vision.

From 1961 to 1979, M. Y. Chan worked in a night soil pit in China. That meant he spent six to eight hours a day standing in human excrement with no protection, filling buckets with waste to be spread on fields as fertilizer. Not a fun gig. The huge prison camp in Kiangsu province had four main latrine areas, and they all drained into one horrendous hellhole, where he stood every day in sludge sometimes up to his waist.

Chan was singled out for this punishment as a Chinese pastor with a church of 300. He survived those 18½ years without one sick day, and his church grew to 5,000 in his absence. Now 58, he has churches in 20 locations, each with about 1,000 believers.

If your pastor was sent to prison for his Christian stand, would it have the same multiplying effect on your people? Of course, you don't want him to go to prison. But you do want your people to see themselves as an integral part of the exciting things God is doing in your community. It will revolutionize them.[3]

Helping a Group Get Pregnant

Before a small group can give birth to a new group, it must get pregnant. That's a fact of life! So here are a few ways to help a group get pregnant.

1. Include a prayer in each week's meeting for those who will go out of their group to help start a new one. This is another way of communicating vision. It gives the Holy Spirit an additional opportunity to work with the hearts of potential leaders.

2. If more than 10 people are in attendance, break into smaller groups for prayer—more people can pray and be prayed for. They discover the Lord is with them as much as He is with the entire group.

3. Give away leadership responsibility to people in the group, such as in leading the prayer time, leading part of the lesson, welcoming guests, planning a special event, and phoning regular attenders and prospects. They will receive immediate affirmation from the group and are being trained without realizing it.

When a group is ready to multiply, it is very much

like a family having a child leave. It is happy and sad at the same time—happy because you have been able to do what you set out to do, and sad because your group will miss them. The ones going out to start a new group will be your best people. Praise the Lord! The goal will always be to raise them up and send them out. But don't divide a "family." That would not be a loving thing to do.

Seven Steps for Birthing a New Group

1. Complete as much of a plan sheet as possible, and keep working on the blanks that need to be filled.

Group leader _____

Apprentice leader _____

Host/Hostess _____ Phone _____

Address where the group will meet _____

_____

Starting date _____

Regular meeting time: Day of week _____ Time _____

Number on the responsibility list so far_____

2. Schedule an appointment with the pastor, who will "coach" the leaders of the new group. The pastor may be able to help fill in some of the blanks and suggest prospects who can be contacted.

3. Begin building a responsibility list with the names, addresses, and phone numbers of people already contacted by the leadership team (leader, apprentice leader, host/hostess).

Other sources of prospects:

- The best prospects for a small group that wants to grow are from the people who are already active in it. These would include family, neighbors, work associates, and friends.

- First-time and returned visitors at the church are hot prospects. Whether they are churched or unchurched when they come through the doors of the building, something has happened in their lives that has brought them to you. By their attendance and giving their names and other information, they have indicated the fact that they are on a spiritual search.

- Membership classes are another great source of group prospects. They are making faith commitments in their lives and need the fellowship of a group to help them. It is impossible to relate to a large group. Besides, the church is not an audience.

- Occasionally a special emphasis may be given in a public service about what happens in our groups. A few curious ones will indicate an interest, and immediate follow-up may result in a prospect. But this source is not as fertile as the other three.

* * *

A Five-Minute Start for a Successful Small Group
(All questions should be answered with a "yes.")

1. Are you interested in helping start a small group?

2. Will you commit one hour each week to help make this group successful?

3. Do you know three other people who could join with you in the future?

Note: You and your 3 guests plus each of their 3 guests total a group of 13 people already. It's as easy as one, two, three!

Their guests

Your guests

You

* * *

4. Pray for those on the responsibility list to keep them warm and to inspire you to make phone calls and home visits as the Lord directs.

5. Give tender loving care to the people on the responsibility list. Working the list will keep it alive and active. This responsibility can be shared by others in the group, but ultimately it will happen only if the leader or leader-couple is leading by example.

6. Keep a few principles in mind, using the multiplication sketch for reference, *(a)* Although it is not always possible, it is best when the leader of the "mother group" goes out to start the new group, leaving the senders under the leadership of the apprentice who has been raised up. This gives a strong message that the group is not leader-centered. *(b)* The new group and the "mother group" both need a team of leaders in place to continue to be healthy. Some or all of the leadership for the new group may come from the original group. But they will prospect their own people. *(c)* The groups and leaders who are "birthed" by a reproducing group will always be related. They will celebrate each other's victories and growth. They will meet together occasionally for special events. *(d)* Every baby is different, even though they have many things in common. Every birth is different in the delivery room as well as in the multiplication of groups, but the principles are common. *(e)* Contractions can be expected and should not come as a surprise. Some mothers have very slight discomfort; for others it is severe and very painful. So it is with birthing groups. But no matter what has been experienced, the new life is cause for celebration!

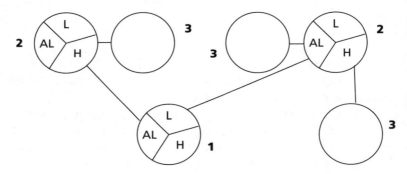

7. For a successful start, we suggest that the first meeting be a social event for people to get acquainted, to have fellowship with a meal or dessert, and to hear a brief description by the leader about what the purpose of the weekly small group will be. This would be an excellent time for the leader (and others) to share what a group experience has meant to them. Invite everyone to come back the next week and bring others with them as the group begins following the suggested order of a group (pp. 99-100) and following the discussion guide provided by the pastoral staff.

The Length of a Pregnancy

There are several factors that will determine the length of a group's pregnancy: vision, love, maturity, evangelism, prayer, and so on. Through the years we have noticed that the average is about 6 months. Some groups will be ready to birth a new group in 3 or 4 months, but some will need 9 to 12 months to raise up leaders who can take new responsibility in another circle of love. It is not the size of the group that determines its ability to multiply; it is its health.

❦ 11

How to Develop
Specialty Groups

The church is the best place of all in a community to open the doors for groups of people who need intervention and ongoing help. To offer this kind of help would fit the mission statement of almost every church I know. And when these groups are in place, good things continue to happen in people's lives and in their families. Also, benefits will come to the pastor (with a lighter counseling load) and to the church (whose people can be referred *in* rather than to an outside agency).

Other churches and pastors in the community can also benefit for the same reasons. There seems to be no place better than the church for meeting the desperate needs of our people, such as alcohol and drug abuse, separation and divorce, remarriage, grief, eating disorders, emotional disabilities, co-dependence, sexual addiction and abuse, debt, and terminal illness.

God's people who have had similar life experiences are the best of all the people in a community to reach out loving hands. They are able not only to give factual information and mutual support but also to lift up Jesus, who is our Healer/Counselor/Provider/Deliverer. The twelve-step programs (which have helped so many people through the years) are spiritual journeys, and the ones who have experienced God's grace seem to be the best qualified to lead the journey. They are the best qualified to say, "God gives victory over _____ in your life."

More and more church leaders are discovering that recovery and support groups serve as a wonderful outreach to the unchurched and their families (who are probably unchurched). When God's love is generously given, needs are being met, hurts are being healed, emptiness is being filled, accurate information is being given, new hope is being realized—bringing a person to faith in Christ is easy. God's unconditional love has melted whatever defenses may have been there before.

It Starts in the Heart

How does a church get started in specialty small-group ministry? By a decision coming out of the church office or a committee? No! But isn't that what offices and committees are supposed to do?—make a decision about meeting this need, buy a bunch of books, and recruit a group leader, who gets the teacher's manual? No, the beginning and the developing of multiplied special needs groups will come about because the Holy Spirit is at work in the hearts of God's people.

It starts in the heart of a pastor or a church leader, who then communicates the vision to others. God gives visions that will always be bigger than the person receiving them. So for the vision to be fulfilled, help from others is required. This process will take some time, as explained in chapter 6, "How to Get Started with a Pilot Group."

Also, for many churches the start-up time is going to be delayed because they have forgotten how to love.

They have preached God's blazing judgment down on the alcoholics, the chemically dependent, the divorced, the violently angry, the sexually perverted, the debt-paralyzed until they need some time to learn how to love again. They cannot suddenly open their church doors and say to these desperately hurting people, "Welcome! Come on in!" More than an announcement in the church bulletin, God's unconditional love will bring the people.

The pastor's role is unique in putting this kind of ministry into place. He or she probably has not personally experienced alcohol and drug abuse, sexual perversion and abuse, or divorce and remarriage and therefore has trouble relating to these desperate needs. The pastor has compassion and mercy gifts and access to a variety of resources that are available, such as published material, videos, local agencies, mental health professionals, and seminars. But the greatest resource will be the people God has already given (or will bring to) the church. The pastor gives the people his or her blessing and permission, along with the resources to help them be successful in *their* ministry.

Besides the pastor and church having this vision for special needs groups, the Holy Spirit will also start in the heart of a leader. The leader will have the same qualifications as other small-group leaders (see Appendix 1) but will help others through his or her own life experience. Who is there in your church right now who has experienced God's grace in a specific area of his or her life? It was painful, but God healed. It was ugly, but God restored. It was broken, but God reconciled. Please don't make the well-intentioned mistake of holding that person away from ministry until he or she is *completely* healthy and whole. That will happen for all of us only when we cross the threshold into heaven!

I'll never forget my first visit to an Alcoholics Anonymous group. A friend of mine had told me what wonderful help he had received there to overcome his alcohol addiction. I jumped at the chance when he invited me. Such genuine concern, such mutual support (because they were in recovery together), such good information about what they were confronting, such love and acceptance, such honesty! Except for the cigarette smoke that filled the room, I absolutely loved being there with him and wished I could go every Saturday night!

On our way home he asked me to comment on the evening, and I told him I could certainly understand why that group meeting was so important to him. I told him I enjoyed meeting his sponsor and asked if everyone had a sponsor. He said, "Oh, yes, and most of us have someone *we* sponsor. That's how I stay sober! I have someone who has taken responsibility to help me, and he's going to be checking on me. He is committed to me to help me stay sober; he's been sober longer than me. Then I have a man I am committed to help. He's counting on me to make it, because he can't make it on his own."

By the time my friend had explained the sponsor relationship, I was so excited. I was almost screaming, "That's the New Testament plan!" We are all called to give away what we have received (2 Cor. 1:3-4). In fact, that's all we have to give. When it is given away it multiplies.

One more favorite verse needs to be mentioned in this context: Rom. 8:28. As we begin developing leaders for specialty groups, they will celebrate over and over again the truth of that promise. God will work through the pain and brokenness that has left some scars. He will begin working for good as they have the opportunity to help others with a journey they've already made.

The Twelve Steps

The Twelve Steps of Alcoholics Anonymous form the outline of a spiritual journey. They have been adopted by many other organizations to help people recover from compulsive and addictive behaviors. In fact, by taking a close look at the 12 steps, a person can quickly realize how we *all* need to take those steps in our lives. For what purpose? To receive God's salvation! Step one: I must admit I am powerless over the sin in my life. Step two: I put my trust in God. Step three: I turn my will over to Him. And on to the following nine.

As a means of introducing the reader, or for a quick review, each of the 12 steps is listed below, along with some of their biblical complements.

1. *We admitted we were powerless over* _____, *that our lives had become unmanageable.*

   2 Cor. 1:9; Rom. 7:18

2. *We came to believe that a power greater than ourselves could restore us to sanity.*   Prov. 28:26;

   Ps. 103:3-4

3. *We made a decision to turn our will and our lives over to the care of God as we understood Him.*

   Prov. 3:5-6; 1 Pet. 1:8

4. *We made a searching and fearless moral inventory of ourselves.*   Lam. 3:40

5. *We admitted to God, to ourselves, and to another human being the exact nature of our wrongs.*

   James 5:16

6. *We were entirely ready to have God remove all these defects of character.*   Ps. 119:133

7   *We humbly asked him to remove all our shortcomings.*   1 John 1:9

8. *We made a list of all persons we had harmed and became willing to make amends to them all.*   Rom. 13:8

9. *We made direct amends to such people wherever possible, except when to do so would injure them or others.*   Rom. 12:18

10. *We continued to take personal inventory and when we were wrong, promptly admitted it.*   Rom. 12:3

11. *We sought through prayer and meditation to improve our conscious contact with God as we understood Him, praying only for knowledge of His will for us and the power to carry that out.*   Prov. 2:3-5; Rom. 12:2; Ps. 27:1-5

12. *Having had a spiritual awakening as the result of these steps, we tried to carry this message to others in need and practice these principles in all our affairs.*[1]   1 Pet. 3:15

Children's Groups

In developing specialty groups to meet the needs of people described in this chapter, church leaders must include plans for the children. These are family problems. When an adult is chemically dependent, the children are directly affected. When a loved one dies, the children try to cope with the loss. When abuse occurs in a home, the children who are not the victims are influenced negatively by that action. And when Mommy and Daddy are divorced, their children very often get divorced.

In order to care better for the children from these troubled homes, most of the specialty groups would probably meet at the church facility. More rooms would be available where adults with their own life experience can plan special activities and discussions to help the children resolve their own issues.

Caution: Don't wait to help the children until the best curriculum can be found. Healing love is their greatest need; not books and tapes. In our love and in their pain, they find Jesus.

Partial Listing of Specialty Groups

There is no way a complete list can ever be made for all the possible groups a church might develop. It depends on the freedom that the Holy Spirit has to move in the hearts of God's people and then for those visions to be translated into strategy. Again, the beginning step is for God to raise up a person who has had some life experience in the area in which he or she now wants to help others.

There are three basic categories of specialty groups; a *partial* list will be given in each so creativity will flow and visions can be conceived.

Recovery Groups

Grief Recovery	Violent Anger
Separation Survival	Alcohol Abuse
Divorce Recovery	Drug Dependency
Sexual Addictions	Eating Disorders
Sexual Abuse	Tobacco Addiction

Support Groups

Parenting	Grandparenting
Step-parenting	Infertile Couples
Remarriage	Families of Prisoners

Marriage Enrichment
Marriage Reconciliation
Widows and Widowers
Terminally Ill

Caregivers *(both family
and professionals who
care for the confined)*
Men
Ladies
Emotionally Disabled

Age-groups

Children
Youth
Senior Adults

Young Singles
Older Singles
"Sandwich Generation"
*(those with children at
home who also care for
their elderly parents)*

Prospecting New Members

We are discovering an amazing evangelical wave in churches that develop specialty groups. The percentage of people who attend these groups and do not yet know Jesus is very high. They come because of their powerlessness over whatever they are struggling with, and while surrounded with His love they find Him to be the answer! Their group is their entry point—church attendance will come later for them.

Every church has a front door and a back door. The front door is for those who attend the big events; the back door is for people who decide to leave us for whatever reason. What we provide for our people in specialty groups is a "side door" ministry.

Prospecting new members for these groups is relatively easy because of two factors. One is that when God has done a mighty work in a person's life, his or her friends and family will be the first to know it—and the chances are very high that they are struggling with the same issues. It is no surprise when they also walk through the church doors into the arms of Jesus. One of the reasons evangelism seems difficult for some churches is because their people no longer have meaningful contacts with the unsaved.

The other reason prospecting is easy for specialty groups is because we all have these needs; both Christians and non-Christians are affected by these issues. If I am a parent of school-age children, I know other parents who face the same challenges. If I am suffering the loss of a loved one, there are others around me with the same need. If I am addicted to drugs and alcohol, I probably have spent time with people who struggle with the same things.

As an illustration, I am reminded of a group I helped organize for retired men. Five of us met around a table at a restaurant for lunch. We discussed the challenges of daily life, prayed for each other, and started to set the date for the next meeting. Our thought was to meet once each month, and in almost one voice they asked, "Why do we have to wait a month? Why can't we meet next Monday?—we don't have anything else to do!" The next week eight men were at the table. The retired knew the retired and brought them into the fellowship because of common need.

Specialty Group Objectives

Although the needs met in specialty groups are the same as those in all small groups, we need to emphasize them here in order to understand the vital role of specialty groups. People who are facing the challenges listed in this chapter are commonly feeling disorientation and/or confusion, their self-esteem and personal worth has been battered, and they feel inadequate and incapable of restructuring their lives. Therefore, they need the hidden power of friends more than at any other time in their lives. Many will have experienced some isolation because their family and friends don't understand what they're going through. Social contacts with people who are also "on the journey" will become very valuable. When they are given the opportunity to express their complex emotions, help is on the way. If they can talk it out, the chances are good that they can work it out.

Both Christians and non-Christians who wrestle with these issues are going to need a safe harbor. And that's a pretty good description of a specialty group— *safe harbor*. Words of praise, words of hope, words of encouragement, words of affirmation, and words of acceptance are the order of the day.

Objectives include

1. Helping set individual, realistic goals by receiving the perspectives of others in the group.

2. Gaining self-control over unwanted habits and thoughts.

3. Receiving a higher motivation to do what's right.

4. Increasing self-worth based on who we are in Christ—created in God's image and led by the Holy Spirit.

Guidelines for Specialty Groups

As in the objectives, these guidelines are the same as for other small groups. Because of the openness of the groups and the number of people who come and go, some leaders will want to print these guidelines on a handout for each week's meeting.

1. The leader will have an agenda for group interaction but also will have an ear to the Holy Spirit's leading.

2. The information shared in the group will be kept confidential. What we say here stays here!

3. We will strive for 100-percent participation; everyone who desires to share will have the opportunity.

4. One-to-one praying will be done by members of the same sex.

5. No one will be permitted to do all the talking.

6. No one will be permitted to confess anyone else's faults but his or her own.

7. No one (not even the leader) has all the answers. The group is learning and growing together. We depend on the Holy Spirit to draw the final conclusion as it perfectly fits each individual's needs.

I challenge every local church to raise up leaders with valuable life experiences who will give God's grace and His love away. Jesus said we have freely received and to give to others in the same way. The promise for all of us who are "on the journey" is from the apostle Paul to the Philippians (1:6): God "who has begun a good work in you will carry it on to completion."

❀ 12

How to Plan a Training Event
for New Leaders

Since small-group ministry is the mobilization of lay leaders, one of the most often-asked questions is "Where do we find the leaders?" And when that question is answered, the follow-up question is "How do we train them?" The answer to both questions is the same: *in the groups.* That is almost too simple; we stumble over its wisdom.

It is by design that the training chapter appears toward the close of this book. That's because this is *not* the starting place for local church leaders who want to develop a network of small groups. That strategy is in

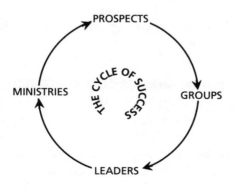

chapter 6. As illustrated in "The Cycle of Success" (p. 157), the leaders who come to a training event will be coming from groups. So we are not presenting our material to prospective leaders who are cold. They have already been trained in group life and have a good idea about the responsibility of leaders. Our goal, then, is to fine-tune and perfect what they already know.

The greatest temptation to be avoided is to make the training event a class. If we yield to that temptation, we will send out teachers of classes, because that is what we did when we trained them. We must plan a training event that is a group experience as much as possible, avoiding the academics. Those needs are best met in the education ministries of the church.

Perhaps it would be helpful to review the qualifications we seek in the leaders of our small groups. Primarily they are *caregivers* who distinguish themselves by being "FAT" (**F**aithful, **A**vailable, **T**eachable). The leaders God gives us will each have a combination of interests and spiritual gifts, but all will have one desire: to give God's love away, to love people God's way. In helping our people develop ministry skills, we are in effect helping them develop parenting skills. Paul illustrated this in 1 Thess. 2 when he referred to himself as a mother, as a father, and as a brother. This is a relational ministry. Therefore, the training event should be what we want to reproduce.

Jesus' On-the-Job Training

Jesus used a method for training His disciples that was far different from what we keep trying to do today. He did not sit them down in a sterile classroom away from the real needs of people. No, He showed them and sent them out and would not let them rest with success or failure. He promised them the Holy Spirit would supervise their ministry after He was gone. Today when we look at His method, we gasp and our mouths fall open. We say things like, "But they don't know enough!" That's true. How much do they need to know? Answer: "I don't know!"

Have you wondered how we have strayed away from doing it the way Jesus did it? I have. I have decided that we do our primary training of pastors in a classroom, and when those pastors go out to train their people, they do what was done to them—put them in a classroom and tell them what they need to know.

Jesus let His men have some experiences and express their opinions, and then He confirmed or corrected before sending them out again. He even let them fail. When they did, it helped Jesus to be more specific in His training.[1]

All of the above is to help us know that in the training of a skill of any kind we need practice. This is true in athletics, music, math, computers, and, yes, even ministry. Surveys by the dozens have proved the value of practice over simple hearing. After 30 days people will remember only 10 percent of what they heard, 50 percent of what they saw, 70 percent of what *they* said, and 90 percent of what they did. So, to reach the higher percentages, we need to train our people with a process—and not just in one concentrated event.

The Process

Step one: "I do—you watch"
Step two: "I do—you assist"
Step three: "You do—I assist"
Step four: "You do—I watch"[2]

It is obvious to the leader that I am in favor of a

training process over a training event. The weekly training events are explained in chapter 8. However, there will need to be a few concentrated training events in the course of a church year. These will be open to everyone who is interested in small-group ministry, and no commitment is required *before* the training. It is a popular mistake to recruit people to the leadership of a small group before they understand what they are committed to. The best recruiters of new leaders will be group leaders who have watched the progress of their people. They have observed their relational skills as they interacted with the group. They have seen their spiritual growth and their discovery of ministry gifts. And now comes the payoff of the leader's faithful ministry, when he or she sees new people coming forward to serve. Quite often the leader will accompany his or her recruit to the training event. What a thrill for both—and what rejoicing also takes place in heaven!

A Suggested Schedule

Since the training is not primarily an academic activity and the trainees have already experienced group life, we are not going to need an exhaustive course. Don't make the mistake of trying to teach everything they will ever need to know before they get to do this ministry. Even if we *could* (and that would be impossible), all the potential "what ifs" would be so overwhelming that the trainees would quit right on the spot. Small-group ministry is really not complicated. God continues to do extraordinary things through the lives of ordinary people who are "FAT." As leaders, we simply give them some tools to work with and sharpen the tools they already have.

The schedule I am *suggesting* is the very minimum.

Even though we will probably use a workbook to help us stay on track, we could never accomplish our objectives if we had 13 weeks of lessons prepared. Three hours is not enough to train our leaders adequately, but 30 hours would still not be enough. Training is a process more than an event. Remember: starting this ministry in a local church is not going to happen in a class, but rather in a pilot group (chapter 6).

Saturday Morning

Let your interested people know that the training will be from nine to noon on Saturday but to come early for fellowship. That will send a strong message along with the invitation that this is going to be more than another class, another "sit there and listen" type of morning.

8:30   Fellowship with coffee, juice, fruit, doughnuts, muffins, and so on.

9:30   Gather around a table so everyone can see and be seen, hear and be heard. If the table is not big enough, arrange the chairs in a circle and treat it like a giant small group. Make sure everyone is introduced with first names only. Perhaps you'd like to let them visit enough so that each could introduce the person on his or her right with the person's first name and one thing the group would like to know about him or her. After the introductions, invite comments from those who want to share about their experiences in a small group. A question to spark the sharing would be something like, "What has been added to your life by participating in a small group?" Some may also want to share about the reason they are attending this training event.

9:30 *Leaders.* "The believer's fourfold call to ministry" (below) can be discussed with the accompanying verses—but no sermonizing! Personal stories will make each point meaningful, such as naming the significant people God has brought into our lives who have been missionary, ambassador, shepherd, and/or servant to us.

Missionary—Matt. 28:18-20
Ambassador—2 Cor. 5:19-20
Shepherd—John 21:15-17
Servant—Matt. 20:28 and Rom. 12:11[3]

The objective is to establish the fact that real ministry is not reserved for just a few who are professionally trained.

These spiritual qualifications are followed by the five "qualities of a leader" that are essential. There is no substitute for any of these five; if any one is missing, the leader is not going to be effective. The best way to measure leadership is to notice if anyone is following!

Enthusiasm	Believing that nothing is impossible with God, no matter what the circumstances might be.
Clear Testimony	Having a clear witness to what Christ has done in your life.
Dedication	Being committed to the mission of the church and the building of people in small groups.
Spirit-led Life	Being sensitive and submissive to the Holy Spirit's lead-

	ership by daily fellowship with Him.
Time and Means	Not being encumbered with life's problems that are of a magnitude that dealing with them is like bondage.

A quick look at Exod. 18:17-27 will help the trainees see their importance in the total life of the church by caring for about 10 people beyond themselves. This will be clarified even more by seeing how leadership in a small group is a team effort (leader, apprentice, host). Job descriptions (such as those in the Appendix) can be distributed at this time.

10:15 Break

10:30 *Groups.* Since we are training leaders to facilitate discussion in a group, we want to demonstrate that as well as telling them. The four principles for growing healthy groups (chap. 7) will need to be studied and practiced.

> Principle No. 1—Balance
> Principle No. 2—Participation
> Principle No. 3—Loving Response
> Principle No. 4—Follow-up

While discussing the need for conversational prayer, the best thing to do is to pray. Give a few guidelines, and then ask what concerns they might have for the group to pray about. Share and pray and teach all at the same time. Remember: we are not training teachers to teach lessons to students. We are training caregivers who are helping people to grow up in their faith. The lesson itself is an important part of that growth, but it is more a discussion guide than a research tool.

11:30   *Accountability.* The weekly huddle meeting with leaders is discussed and the reasons given for its importance. This is outlined in chapter 8. The weekly report sheets (in the Appendix) are discussed and the reasons why we need to communicate with each other as Jesus' disciples did in Mark 6:30. Then, the very last thing to do is give everyone the opportunity to fill out the commitment sheet (sample in the Appendix). An opportunity for a group prayer needs to be given before the commitments are made. Answer all questions so the commitments that are made are done so with full disclosure.

11:45   *Sharing.* As people hand in their commitment sheets, they should be encouraged to share with the group about God's call in their lives. They can talk about new groups they want to help birth. They can talk about being apprentices in the groups they are already in. They can talk about brand-new ideas for ministries for which there is presently no strategy. All their sharing will encourage not only the group but also their own resolve to be used of God in a mighty way.

Before closing this chapter I must include a wonderful letter that came after I had conducted a small-group conference that included a number of churches. Pastor Kent Rogers writes from Campbell River, British Columbia:

Dear Floyd,

Thank you for a very enjoyable and informative seminar. My wife and I were challenged in many areas of our church life. I believe you have identified and put into operation the missing part of most church methods: namely, the effective training of lay people.

I have two brothers-in-law who are grain farmers. Once I arrived in their area for a visit and they were short a grain truck driver. They quickly pressed me into service, and just as quickly gave me instructions on how to drive the truck, pick up the grain from the combines, drive back to the granary, lift the box, start the auger, and lower the box. I, finally, in frustration, told them that if they expected me to drive their truck, they had better train me.

Once again, thank you for a most rewarding time.

Kent Rogers

The training Kent was requesting was to help him do what he was already doing—he wanted to do it better. How foolish it would have been to put him into a classroom with a manual filled with policies and procedures about trucks and combines and augers. There was grain to be gathered and delivered before harvesttime was past. That almost sounds like something I read in the Bible!

The watchword for a training event for new leaders is this: "It is not us pulling them together, but helping them to pull together."

❀ 13

How to Write
Dialogue Questions

"We believe the spiritual direction of a local church is accomplished through the anointed preaching of the Word of God."

If the reader agrees with that statement, then to provide discussion questions each week from the same Scripture passage that the pastor used would be a great asset. When multiple groups are using the same discussion guide, there are several very positive advantages. I'll name just a few.

- The truth proclaimed in the Sunday sermon is dialogued and prayed about and is more apt to be applied than if it was only heard.
- Group members interact with God's Word (not the pastor's sermon) in such a personal way that they can be accountable to each other as they put its truths into their lives.
- The lesson guide is provided so group leaders are not required to develop their own lessons each week.
- Since the leaders are only facilitating discussion, they do not have to do homework in preparation for a "class."

- As groups begin to multiply, they are easier to supervise if they are all going in the same direction.
- By all going in the same direction (except for the specialty groups), the church will experience momentum as they move toward common goals.

The Need for a Lesson Guide

There are dozens of ways God's Word can be communicated in a small group. Which one is the best? Answer: All of them, because of the promise of Isa. 55:11 that His Word will not return empty. Notice that He did not make that promise about what *we* say His Word says.

In the context of a relational group where we commit ourselves to grow together more than just to get smart together, the need for a simple discussion guide is very evident. Let's look at it first from the leader's point of view. By having a few questions on a half sheet of paper, the leader can help the group stay on track. Once in a while, comments will be made that are untrackable. If the leader senses a discussion loop that is not going anywhere, all he or she needs to do is say, "Thank you. Now let's go on to question number four." The group looks at their paper, and together they move forward again. The goal of the group and the leader is not to "do the lesson." The group goal is to meet the needs of the people. The lesson becomes a vehicle to help them reach that destination, avoiding the cul-de-sacs that can become dead ends.

Now let's look at the lesson guide from the viewpoint of the Holy Spirit. God's Word is given to us to change our lives, not just to have some more information to think about. The questions at the close of a lesson are personal commitment questions. Those are the most important ones according to the Spirit. He would be grieved if scripture was discussed and not applied to daily life.

From the group member's point of view, a half-sheet discussion guide can be tucked easily into the Bible that is opened on his or her lap. Everyone receives the sheet as he or she comes to the meeting. To have it earlier than that would cause some to do homework and tell everyone else what they learned. The total learning would go down if the group only listened to what a few had learned. Many published Bible studies are available, but most tend to be content-oriented and are more conducive to the education ministry of the church. When other books are studied, the Bible is relegated to a reference position rather than the source.

Finally, we need to look through the eyes and sense with the spirit of a first-time guest in a group. If people are into the middle of a book study, the first-time guest is lost because he or she hasn't read the book. If people are sitting around with the questions already answered (the blanks already filled), it's just too intimidating. It's like sitting in the penalty box or being the "dumb freshman." By giving an academic emphasis to a lesson presented by a teacher-type, only students will attend. Even people who enjoy reading and studying will stay away from on-going evening classes. Their hearts desire healing fellowship. The first-time guest will feel very comfortable when he or she realizes everyone (including the leader) is on the same page as they share their inside journey.

The Language of Relationship

Have we put too much faith in the use of words? I know I have when my wife says something like "That wasn't a nice thing to say!" When I ask what it was that wasn't nice, she responds, "It wasn't *what* you said—it was *how* you said it." Throwing words at each other alone would not build relationship. We need the language of relationship, which is dialogue.

It is a most wonderful moment when two people can communicate with their hearts. Words are used, but they carry only what is in their hearts. The sharing and the listening are done with an accepting of the "otherness" of the other person.

The goal for our small group is to give the opportunity for everyone to enter into dialogue, including the Holy Spirit. This could be a big challenge for people who have been hurt with words in their past and they come into the group with injured spirits. Their receptors need healing. Others have learned to protect themselves with their mouths and will frequently say things with little or no regard for how it lands.

I am convinced the best place in all the world for both of these kinds of people is the small group. In a climate of love, we all learn to listen with our hearts and share from our hearts. We become more open and authentic, willing to reveal what God is doing inside us. We speak with conviction about certain issues but validate the convictions of others too. We celebrate the oneness we have in Christ at the same time we acknowledge our differences. Yes, even in those times when the words seem to be in competition, we can create a bonding by a tone of voice and a facial expression.

Dialogue builds cohesiveness, and cohesiveness is the key to growth and success of a small group. That cohesive element can be felt as soon as a first-time guest walks in. I cannot fully explain it, but I know what it feels like. Cohesiveness in a group seems to give a form of energy to each member. Members are better able to resolve conflicts in their personal lives. The healing oil of the Holy Spirit touches deeper needs in a "together" group. They also have a higher attendance commitment than groups who are still learning to trust each other. It is not an accident that this paragraph describes a healthy family. After all, the family was God's original small group.

Dialogue Gives Life to the Group

In all the relationships of life, the flowing of communication from one to another and back again is what makes it meaningful. This process called "dialogue" is as important as blood is to the body—there is no life in a relationship without it. Our goal in group life is to provide maximum opportunity for dialogue to flow—not only from the leader to each member and back, but from each member to each member and back again. It's just another reason why effective groups are small.

We also want the Bible to enter into this miracle of dialogue. Instead of the leader and/or the author of the lesson telling us what the Bible says, the Bible is able to speak for itself to every member if we let it. Our goal is to provide discussion questions that not only help group members talk to each other but also that are answered directly from the Bible.

Principles for Effective Lesson Guides

1. Life-centered. Since our goal is Bible application, the lesson guide we want to use needs to be practical and personal in the way it's put together. To do a series of lessons on the Trinity, for example, would be wonderful for a class to study, but not in a small group. Why? Because our people need to know about the Trinity (in a class), but they can't go out and *do* one. The

Word of God is studied in a small group, but it is life-centered more than an academic exercise. The education ministry of the church provides for that.

2. Good questions. Good lesson guides have good questions—and good questions are the kind that cannot be answered yes or no. We want our people to talk to each other about the Scripture passage, and if a question is answered yes or no, that's the end. There is no discussion (unless, of course, a "Why?" is attached). As a general rule, every lesson guide will have three kinds of questions designed in such a way that everyone gets into the discussion early, participation stays high with the Bible, and it closes with personal commitment to applicable truth. The three kinds of questions are as follows:

> a. *Nonthreatening.* Everyone in the group can answer these, because every answer is the right answer. The Bibles have not been opened yet, but the opening questions help direct the thoughts of the people toward the topic of the lesson. Even the first-time guest, a child, or a person who is not yet acquainted with the Bible can answer a nonthreatening question. (Refer to the sample lesson that follows, questions 1-2.)
>
> b. *Biblical.* Since we want the Bible to enter into the dialogue, we must write questions that will allow that. To write a question from two verses of scripture that asks, "What does this mean to you?" would not be allowing the Bible to speak. We would answer that question from our heads, and how much can be learned from that source? A better question from those same two verses would be, "What are the three things Jesus said to do in these two verses?" Immediately you see everyone's eyes

focus on God's Word, and the answers come from it. Sometimes we have people who want to change or add to what the Bible says. We need to help our leaders learn to dialogue with the Bible and interact with it. A helpful response to an "addition" would be "That seems like a good thing, but that's not what it says here. Now, of these three things Jesus said for us to do, which one is the most difficult for you to put into your life?" And immediately all the eyes focus on the open Bibles, and the Holy Spirit is at work. (Refer to the sample lesson that follows, questions 3-5.)

c. *Personal.* Some of the questions need to probe into what the people have experienced, are experiencing, or would like to experience. These questions are important throughout the discussion as we share life with each other but are especially helpful at the close. They bring us to a place of encouraging each other to commit the truth to our daily lives in prayer. We discover again that God's Word changes us. To answer a personal question helps a person to go public with his or her search for significant faith. (Refer to the sample lesson that follows, questions 6-7.)

3. Questions answer questions. It is always enjoyable when a written question on a discussion guide raises other questions. Instead of the question-writer trying to think of every possible one, the questions he or she does write form a guide for the ones generated from the group. New questions are asked in groups where freedom reigns. If tension is present, people tend to keep their personal questions to themselves.

Caution: Except for the "biblical" questions, try to avoid the questions that have only one answer: the author's. These tend to be demoralizing in a group, because every answer given gets the buzzer except the right one. After a while no one wants to respond because he or she doesn't want the wrong-answer buzzer to go off.

4. Lesson guide preparation. Many churches and pastors are discovering the power of writing their own lesson guides from the same Scripture passage they used for Sunday's sermon. There are many advantages, and it is not really that hard. Notice that I did not say the lesson is from the sermon. It is from the scripture that also inspired the sermon. So the pastor, while putting the sermon together, has a piece of paper to the side for questions he or she would love to dialogue with the congregation, but that's not the forum for discussion. Sermons are monologues, groups are dialogues, and the pastor makes the most of both opportunities by connecting them. Remember, as carefully as you prepare the lesson, it will be only a *vehicle* to help meet the needs of your people. Our goal is to connect them with God's life-changing power, not just with our ideas. This is why we work toward creating a climate of love in the group. There is no substitute for the cohesive dynamic in a group's ability to dialogue.

SAMPLE LESSON
Putting Love into Action

1. What are some of the things a person can do to let you know he or she really cares for you?
2. What are some of the things that cause you trouble in your relationships with your friends and family?

3. Read Rom. 12:9-13. In the first part of verse 9, what is the high-priority quality the apostle Paul says love must have? In the second part of verse 9, Paul tells us to do what?

4. When conflicts and problems arise between two people, how can this scriptural truth be put into practice?

5. Read verse 10 in unison: "Love each other with brotherly affection and take delight in honoring each other" (Rom. 12:10, TLB). What are some ways to honor people who are younger than you? Those who are your age? Those who are older?

6. Read verses 11-13 again. Of the commands listed here, which *two* are the easiest for you to keep? Which *one* seems to be the most difficult to keep?

7. Before our next meeting, how can each of us put love into action in our homes, places of employment, neighborhoods, and so on? Let's be specific: "I can put my love into action by . . ."

🌸 14

How to Avoid Seven
Popular Mistakes

Over the years I have answered hundreds (probably thousands) of sincere questions about small-group ministries. After more than two hours of questions and answers one day, a pastor said, "Thank you, Floyd, for your time and for all the help you've given. I have one more question: If you were moving to southern California to develop small groups at a new church, what common mistakes would you avoid?" No one had ever asked it that way before. As I answered him, he carefully took notes. I was so impressed with my answer that I asked him for a copy of what he had written! I realized it formed a summary of what I believe so strongly.

These are very popular mistakes. Some are quite obvious; some are subtle. They remind me of a framed poster that hung in the office where I worked during my college days:

> **PROFIT BY THE MISTAKES
> OF OTHERS**
> because you and I
> in our lifetime
> cannot make them all

Of course, there is no benefit from other churches' mistakes unless we are teachable. *Lord, grant us a teachable spirit.*

1. Avoid an unemployed Holy Spirit. This is a spiritual work. It is directed by the Holy Spirit, not by a church office. If we yield to the Holy Spirit as our Senior Partner, He will direct, He will create, He will raise up, He will heal, He will give courage.

When we teach our people about the person and the ministry of the Holy Spirit, they will see their need to be filled with the Spirit (Acts 1:8), to fellowship with Him (2 Cor. 13:14), and to flow in the power of the Spirit (John 7:38). We need to help our people recognize the ministry of the Holy Spirit in their own lives and in the groups they lead. Living with this reality will bring success to both leaders and groups.

Some of the ministries the Holy Spirit actively performs in a small group are as follows:

- He indwells every believer (Rom. 8:9-11) and therefore is present whenever they gather.
- He guides in the decisions we make (John 16:13) about the truth of the passage we discuss and about how we relate to each other.
- He teaches (John 14:26), and that really takes the pressure off of the leader.
- He convicts us (John 16:8) with personal light about our attitudes and actions that are not pleasing to Him.
- He intercedes for us (Rom. 8:26) when we bring our concerns to God. He knows our deepest needs.
- He enables us (1 Cor. 12:11) to serve the Lord by serving others in unique and special ways.

- He unifies us as members into a body (Eph. 4:3). He does not make us to be the same; He makes us one.

In order for the Holy Spirit to be taken out of the unemployment line, we must be persistent in our prayer life. Things begin to happen when we pray (Acts 4:31-35). Prayer is not only the breath of a believer's life but also the breath of a small group.

2. Avoid a complex organization. It is very important to have a big vision. See multiplied numbers of groups—all kinds of groups. See the multiplication of leaders—all kinds of leaders. But keep the organization simple, simple enough that the ministry can continue to grow without changing everything—like a body. Multiply the cells and raise up leaders with a plan that gives flexibility and mobility.

The organization of the church is like the skeleton of the body. It is there, but it cannot be seen. No one goes around showing off their bones. And when we examine one bone, it appears rigid, and we wonder how it can assist the body. But it is connected to another bone, which is connected to another one. So the body has mobility in the same way the church does when the organization allows for us to work together.

See it big, but keep it simple. Avoid trying to publish a manual with policies and procedures all in place before the first group even meets. Avoid trying to solve every possible problem before the first meeting. Let's invest our energy in the ministry instead of the machinery.

3. Avoid beginning with a class for leaders. Small-group ministry is not another school. If it were, we would begin with a classroom filled with potential teachers. We begin with a small group filled with potential leaders who are caregivers. If we start with a class and tell them what we know, they will go out and do a class and tell them what they should know. This is a relational ministry. There is certainly the dynamic of learning every time we meet, but it is not a teacher/student format. We raise up our people in a "family" atmosphere. When we help develop ministry skills in them, we are actually training them to be "parents" of a small group.

There are some definite principles we are working with, but it is really easier than a lot of models I've seen. Our goal is to enjoy koinonia (the exchanged life) rather than another lesson. Since we are not following an academic model, the best place to learn how to be a small-group leader is in a healthy small group.

4. Avoid stereotyping leaders. Our biggest problem when we recruit leaders is that we look in the wrong places. We look for up-front skills. We look at the leaders we already have. We look to the people who tend to say yes to everything. We look at the outside when God looks at the heart. God gives a variety of ministry abilities and clusters them in each of us as He sees best. And then He groups us together in the church so we can quickly see how much we need each other. No one is above or below another. He wants to use every one of us and to develop us to our full potential. Our God is an economist. He would not give us special ability and then not also provide opportunities for us to serve.

Where I have served, God has brought into lay pastor ministry many leaders whom I would never have chosen—not because they are not good enough but because I tend to look in the wrong places. To illustrate, let me give two brief testimonies from written weekly ministry reports I have received. These are from people who were "discovered" in small groups and then raised up into leadership.

This week I had relatives visit that I don't see very often. Right away I started sharing Christ's love and telling them about becoming a lay pastor. They told me how different I looked and about a glow that I had. Praise the Lord for coming into my life. Both of them are Christians, and it was really wonderful being with them.

* * *

I have a friend who will get out of a treatment center on Friday. She asked me to come to her graduation, and I told her I wouldn't miss it. I pray for her family, that they will be able to adjust to her coming home. I haven't been able to talk to her very much about Jesus, but I did invite her to our small group. I let her know I will always be here for her.

I am so thankful that God uses all of us, and when we work together in concert, extraordinary things happen.

5. Avoid leader-oriented groups. Even though a charismatic-type leader can get a group to grow, it will be weak and anemic. It needs to be life-centered instead of leader-centered.

There are two definite hindrances to a leader-centered group: *(a)* The spiritual growth of the people in the group is kept to a minimum if the leader does the learning and tells the group what he or she learned. They sit and listen. Sitting and listening is only a hindrance to growth. *(b)* New leaders are not going to be raised up and sent out to form new groups, because no one feels adequate to match what the leader does for them every week; he or she is so smooth and has an answer for everything. It's like attending a meeting every week with a guru.

6. Avoid forming a "Holy Club." Sometimes groups start out as a family but before long lose their vision and become a club. There's a lot of difference between a club and a family. Clubs have members and are closed; families have members and are open. New people are actively invited and brought into our circle of love. Before long, they are raised up until they can go out and help start another family. That's multiplication, and God likes multiplication (Matt. 28:18-20).

When the invitation is given, it is not going to be "Come and join our group" but rather "Come and *visit* our group." To join something makes it sound like a closed group, and we want our groups to be open—like a healthy family.

Even specialty groups, which appear to be closed because of the nature of the issues they are confronting, are really open. They exist for a stated series of meetings, and another group is formed for another series. There is always an opening for a person who is seeking help.

7. Avoid starting big. The results will not be good if churches try to get as many people as possible into small groups during a three-month emphasis. We all have had experience and know how our attempt to impose "a new program" on a congregation meets with strong resistance. We know how God wants us to be a body more than an audience. We know this is His design for pastoral care in a local church. We know how we need to develop more disciple-makers. So the temptation is great to preach a sermon about how much we need each other and have everyone sign a card who wants to be in a group. Now—what are we going to do with those cards? We don't have groups yet for those people. And why don't we have groups? Because we don't yet have leaders. And where are we going to get the leaders? From groups—not from the pews.

Start with a big vision and a clear strategy. Start

with a pilot group (or two or three pilot groups) that will be a prototype of the multiplied groups we envision. Grow this ministry up; let it multiply *naturally*. This process of keeping groups healthy and helping them birth leaders and groups will produce the results the Lord wants for us.

I can't even count the number of pastors I have worked with who have become discouraged about small-group ministry. They started with a big training event for leaders, and right away the people they recruited started dropping. They wanted to be in a small group— not a classroom! Some have started with a detailed grid map of their community and tried to assign everyone to a group. Again it's a failure, because people want to go where they want to go. And they go because they were invited (not assigned) to be a part of a "family." We must keep our vision big but start small. Add some patience to a clear strategy, and God will give the increase.

In Conclusion

God wants His people to grow in their faith and to take as many others to heaven as they can. In order to grow in unity and maturity, we all need both the large-group worship and the small-group fellowship. Neither one is a substitute for the other. Both opportunities enrich the other. To put this into a simple equation we have $I + E = G$ and $I - E = D$.

- **Impression**: the large-group celebration event with inspirational singing and a motivating message from God's Word.
- **Expression**: the small-group fellowship with people who are like family. We commit ourselves to put the Scripture into our daily lives with accountability.

- **G**rowth: both individual and corporate growth as we become more and more like our Lord.
- **D**epression: the frustration and alienation that sets in when we worship without personal involvement.

*   *   *

This book provides the ways needed to begin the small-group experience and the tools to see a network of groups become reality. My prayer for every reader has four parts:

- **Warning:** that God would help us not to complicate His design for church life.
- **Challenge:** that every reader would make commitments to a small group of people if he or she is not already active in one.
- **Reminder:** that the Holy Spirit is always active and we yield to Him as to our Senior Partner.
- **Hope:** that church leaders will give away the ministry and as a result grow up a host of disciple-makers in their communities.

Tools

APPENDIX 1
Job Descriptions of Leaders

APPENDIX 2
Commitment Sheet Samples

APPENDIX 3
Accountability Sheet Samples

Appendix 1

Job Descriptions of Leaders

MEET A LAY PASTOR

A lay pastor is a person who has answered the call from God to do the work of ministry. Lay pastors come from all walks of life, all backgrounds, both men and women from all age-groups, from young adults to senior adults. They share a love for God that is grounded in a personal relationship with Jesus Christ and have a clear testimony of His grace in their lives. And because of their love for God, they demonstrate a deep love for people.

Lay pastors schedule their time so they can be with the Lord, growing and preparing themselves for His work. As a result, they fill many roles, not only with the people in their groups, but also in their daily lives:

Friend   Caregiver
Guide   Prayer intercessor
Listener   Sharing brother/sister

Sometimes they're just there to cry with those who cry and rejoice with those who rejoice. They grow in relationships with others and help others grow in their relationships as well.

In all of this, lay pastors do not rely on their own resources; they trust in the Lord to provide in those areas in which they are themselves weak. Lay pastors realize that they are servants of God and that He will never call us to do anything for which He is not willing to equip us.

Lay pastors know they are part of a larger team of people who are all involved in the same kinds of ministries. They receive support from, as well as give support to, the pastoral staff and the other lay pastors in our church.

Please notice that even though our leaders are responsible for what happens in a group meeting (prayer, share, Bible discussion) we do not call them "group leaders." That is by design, not by accident. We want them to become spiritual caregivers in the lives of their people, and *lay pastor* is a good description of that larger ministry. *Group leader* is much too restrictive as a title.

What a Lay Pastor Does

1. A lay pastor is committed to and consistent in living the Christian lifestyle, with a daily discipline of prayer as a top priority.

2. A lay pastor is filled and led by the Holy Spirit.

3. A lay pastor shares the vision of our church and is dependable and accountable to its leadership. He or she is committed to accomplishing the great things God has called us to do together.

4. A lay pastor is a member of the _____ Church, has completed the special lay pastor training, and has been selected by the pastoral staff.

5. A lay pastor participates in a group, either by leading a group or by assisting in the leadership of that group.

6. A lay pastor attends the weekly lay pastors' huddle and brings a written report of his or her personal ministry.

7. A lay pastor comes to the altar to pray with those who come forward.

8. A lay pastor prays faithfully and diligently each week in doing the work God has called him or her to do.

9. A lay pastor is faithful in bringing the Lord His tithe and in giving time.

10. A lay pastor maintains a healthy family life.

MEET A LAY PASTOR CAPTAIN

- Being a lay pastor captain gives lay pastors an opportunity for a deeper level of commitment and a higher level of ministry.
- Being a lay pastor captain provides a natural step for a lay pastor to develop the leadership and pastoral skills to do even greater things for God as he or she grows his or her ministry.
- Lay pastor captains provide our church with the middle management we need in our growing small-group network.
- Lay pastor captains help our coaches effectively manage and produce new growth in their areas of ministry.

Profile

1. Has a vision for small-group ministries and the importance of middle-management people.
2. Radiates enthusiasm and looks for God's best in every person.
3. Demonstrates leadership qualities in relationships with people.
4. Is a growing Christian who models the Christ life.
5. Has been a producer of spiritual growth and a reproducer of leaders and groups.
6. Is cooperative and is a team player.
7. Has the time and interest to do the extra work of supervision.

Job Description

1. Continues to do the things a lay pastor does and more.

2. Supervises the ministry of not more than five lay pastors and helps them be successful. The people on his or her team will be a combination of those he or she has recruited and trained, as well as lay pastors who may be assigned to him or her.

3. Supervises the groups led by his or her team members and helps make those groups healthy.

4. Leads his or her own group and continues to raise up leaders from his or her ministry.

5. Looks for potential leaders and recruits them for the next lay pastor training event.

6. Gives pastoral care to each team member and provides generous amounts of encouragement along with directive suggestions.

7. Initial training will take place at an annual lay pastor captain event. Continual on-the-job training will be under the guidance of his or her coach.

8. The captain will give a weekly ministry report (just as their lay pastors do), with a brief comment of his or her contact with team members.

MEET A LAY PASTOR COACH

- A lay pastor coach can be either salaried or volunteer.
- A lay pastor coach works directly with the pastoral staff in the building of small-group ministries.
- A lay pastor coach has special interest and skills in his or her specific area of ministry: neighborhood, children, youth, special needs, and so on.

Profile

1. Has the ability to recruit, motivate, and train lay pastors and captains so they can be effective in their own ministries.
2. Has a clear vision for our church and for his or her own specific area of ministry.
3. Acts on the fact that nothing is impossible with God.
4. Loves people and gives them generous amounts of tender loving care.
5. Is a soul winner who makes others successful in bringing people to Christ.
6. Has experienced enough trouble and pain to know how to comfort others in theirs.
7. Is a thermostat, not just a thermometer.

Job Description

1. Pastors his or her "church within the church" while serving under the authority of the senior pastor; is loyal and accountable to the senior pastor.
2. Manages the people and resources in his or her area of ministry; fulfills the Great Commission with creativity.

3. Develops the lay pastors and captains on their team to their greatest potential, according to their individual strengths.

4. Gives personal pastoral care to his or her lay pastor captains.

5. Leads the outreach evangelism efforts in his or her area.

6. Sets ambitious goals for recruiting new leaders and creating new groups.

7. Supervises his or her groups and helps them be healthy and prosperous.

8. Strategizes to do in his or her area of ministry what the entire church is endeavoring to do.

MEET A PASTOR OF LAY DEVELOPMENT

Vision
- Sees the big picture of how small groups fit into the total life of the church.
- Is a pioneer (risk-taker) rather than a settler (taking care of what already exists).
- Regularly communicates the importance of small groups to the entire church, as well as through a few high-visibility events each year.
- Strategizes with the other leaders according to his or her God-given vision.

Bible-Based Commitment
- Is willing to work outside traditionally accepted methods but never outside biblical principles.
- Understands that God's design for church life does not allow a gap between clergy and laity.
- Believes undeniably in the priesthood of the believer.
- Is able to help believers discover, develop, and use their spiritual gifts.

Love for People
- Is grace-motivated; quick to love, accept, and forgive.
- Nurtures leaders one-to-one and in small groups with generous amounts of encouragement and affirmation.
- Does not attempt to stereotype leaders.
- Is quick to listen and slow to "quick-fix" people's complex problems.

Team-Player Qualities

- Is a morale booster with the coaches, captains, and lay pastors.
- Not only gives leadership to his or her coaches, captains, and lay pastors but also has a cooperative spirit while working with the senior pastor, the church board, and various committees.
- Is enthusiastic.

Resourcefulness

- Provides both the training opportunities and the materials that are needed.
- Is a teacher with the model given Timothy by the apostle Paul (2 Tim. 2:2).
- Is ready and willing to work with leaders from other churches to help them be successful in small-group ministries led by lay pastors.
- Accepts the responsibility to invest energy and information in an intern.

Management

- Is able to balance his or her own time schedule and help the leaders do the same.
- Delegates responsibility to others according to their interests and abilities.
- Is responsible for the group statistics that measure growth and reports these regularly to the church.

Appendix 2

Commitment Sheet Samples

LAY PASTOR COMMITMENT

1. Today, _____, 19____, I, _____, before my Lord Jesus, commit myself to serve Him and our church by being a lay pastor as together we fulfill our mission to the world.

   Address _____

   _____

   Phone _____ Fax _____

2. As a lay pastor at the _____ (name of church), I commit myself to
   ___ Spend quality time in prayer daily.
   ___ Spend time in the Word daily.
   ___ Be a scriptural tither.
   ___ Be faithful and loyal to the church and to its leadership.
   ___ Allow the Holy Spirit to control my life.
   ___ Attend weekly lay pastor preparation meetings.
   ___ Give a brief weekly report of my ministry.

3. My special area of interest right now is to serve in the following area of ministry:

   Neighborhood group _____

   Special needs group _____

   Specialty group _____

   Children's group _____

   Youth group _____

   Task group _____

   as a

   ___ Group leader

   ___ Apprentice group leader

   Additional comments: _____

   _____

   _____

   _____

   _____

LAY PASTOR CAPTAIN COMMITMENT

1. Today, _____, 19_____, and for the next 12 months, I, _____, before my Lord Jesus, commit myself to serve Him and our church by being a lay pastor captain as together we fulfill our mission to the world.

   Address _____

   _____

   Phone _____ Fax _____

2. As a lay pastor at the _____ (name of church), I will continue to

   ___ Spend quality time in prayer daily.
   ___ Spend time in the Word daily.
   ___ Be a scriptural tither.
   ___ Be faithful and loyal to the church and to its leadership.
   ___ Allow the Holy Spirit to control my life.
   ___ Attend weekly lay pastor preparation meetings.
   ___ Give a brief weekly report of my ministry.

3. As a captain, I will give of myself to help the following lay pastors be successful in their ministry and help supervise the groups they lead.

Name	Group

LAY PASTOR COACH COMMITMENT

1. Today, _____, 19____, and for the next 12 months, I, _____, before my Lord Jesus, commit myself to serve Him and our church by being a lay pastor coach as together we fulfill our mission to the world.
   Address _____

   _____
   Phone _____ Fax _____

2. As a leader at the _____ (name of church), I will continue to
   ___ Spend quality time in prayer daily.
   ___ Spend time in the Word daily.
   ___ Be a scriptural tither.
   ___ Be faithful and loyal to the church and to its leadership.
   ___ Allow the Holy Spirit to control my life.
   ___ Attend weekly lay pastor preparation meetings.
   ___ Give a brief weekly report of my ministry.

3. My vision for our _____ groups is _____
                        (area of ministry)

   _____
   _____
   _____
   _____

   My ministry goals to fulfill this vision in the coming year include

   Lay Pastors   **Groups**
       Present _____   Present _____
       Goal _____   Goal _____
       Total _____   Total _____
   Additional Comments: _____

   _____
   _____
   _____
   _____

PASTOR OF LAY DEVELOPMENT COMMITMENT

1. Today, _____, 19_____, and for the next 12 months, I, _____, before my Lord Jesus, commit myself to serve Him and our church by being a pastor of lay development as together we fulfill our mission to the world.

   Address _____

   _____

   Phone _____ Fax _____

2. As a pastor at the _____ (name of church), I will commit myself to:

   ___ Spend quality time in prayer daily.

   ___ Spend time in the Word daily.

   ___ Be a scriptural tither.

   ___ Be faithful and loyal to the church and to its leadership.

   ___ Allow the Holy Spirit to control my life.

   ___ Attend weekly lay pastor preparation meetings.

   ___ Give a brief weekly report of my ministry.

3. ___ I will communicate vision to our people and develop a strategy that is biblically based and calls forth God's best in our lay pastors.

4. ___ I will give priority time and energy to develop our coaches and captains, because they have the best connection to where the action is.

5. ___ I will give attention to my own personal and family life so I can be in this ministry for the long term.

Appendix 3

Accountability Sheet Samples

Appendix 3

Lay Pastor Weekly Ministry Report

Name _____ Week of _____

Code*	Name*	Code*	Name*

E = Evangelism   L = Letter   D = Discipled
P = Prayer   S = Social   K = Encouragement
C = Counseling   HO = Hospital   PV = Personal Visit
PH = Phone   HE = Helps

****

On a scale of 1 to 10, how would you rate your spiritual walk this week? (Bible reading, prayer, tithing, and so on)

1 2 3 4 5 6 7 8 9 10

****

On a scale of 1 to 10, how would you rate your ministry this week? (Calling members, evangelism, prayer, helping, encouraging, and so on)

1 2 3 4 5 6 7 8 9 10

****

Praise reports, problem areas, answered prayers

_____

_____

_____

_____

*List all group members and the code letter that indicates your involvement with each one between group meetings.

Note: Preparing a personal ministry report is a difficult thing for many people—even for some Christians. They want to serve the Lord, but they want to be independent. To freelance without accountability is very popular. But we're in this together as members in a Body (1 Cor. 12); we need each other. When the team wins, the *whole* team wins. And as coaches (who cannot always be present when ministry is done) we need a report in order to effectively coach the people God has entrusted to our care.

And, by the way, Jesus expected the same for *His* "team."

"The apostles gathered around Jesus and reported to him all they had done and taught" (Mark 6:30).

Weekly Group Report

Meeting Date: _____

Leader: _____

Apprentice Leader: _____

Host: _____

****

Names of Group Attendees

1.   R V RV
2.   R V RV
3.   R V RV
4.   R V RV
5.   R V RV
6.   R V RV
7.   R V RV
8.   R V RV
9.   R V RV
10.   R V RV
11.   R V RV
12.   R V RV
13.   R V RV
14.   R V RV
15.   R V RV
16.   R V RV
17.   R V RV
18.   R V RV
19.   R V RV
20.   R V RV

Totals: __ __ __

On a scale of 1 to 10, rate your group meeting this week: ___

If less than 5, why? _____

_____

R—Regular attender
V—Visitor
RV—Returned visitor

Lay Pastor Captain Weekly Ministry Report

Name _____ Week of _____

Code*	Name*	Code*	Name*

E = Evangelism   L = Letter   D = Discipled
P = Prayer   S = Social   K = Encouragement
C = Counseling   HO = Hospital   PV = Personal Visit
PH = Phone   HE = Helps

****

On a scale of 1 to 10, how would you rate your spiritual walk this week? (Bible reading, prayer, tithing, and so on)

1 2 3 4 5 6 7 8 9 10

****

On a scale of 1 to 10, how would you rate your ministry this week? (Calling members, evangelism, prayer, helping, encouraging, and so on)

1 2 3 4 5 6 7 8 9 10

****

Praise reports, problem areas, answered prayers

_____
_____
_____
_____
_____
_____
_____
_____

*List your group members and the code letter that indicates your involvement with each one between group meetings.

Captain's Report, continued

Lay Pastor Names	Brief report of your contact with them

Total Ministry Report

NEIGHBORHOOD GROUPS	Lay pastors	Group attendance	Visitors and RVs	Responsibility list
TOTAL				
SPECIALTY GROUPS				
TOTAL				
SPECIAL NEEDS GROUPS				
TOTAL				
YOUTH GROUPS				
TOTAL				
CHILDREN'S GROUPS				
TOTAL				
TASK GROUPS				
TOTAL				
GRAND TOTAL				

NOTES

Introduction

1. Jerry Summers, "The Flowering of Chinese Protestant Christianity Since the Cultural Revolution, 1976-1987," *Journal of Religious Studies,* (Spring Quarter 1989): 16.

2. Robert Coleman, *The Master Plan of Evangelism* (Tarrytown, N.Y.: Fleming H. Revell, 1963), 108.

3. Waylon Moore, *Multiplying Disciples* (Colorado Springs: NavPress, 1981), 21-23.

4. Bill Hull, *The Disciple-Making Pastor* (Tarrytown, N.Y.: Fleming H. Revell, 1988), 96.

5. Ibid., 174-76.

6. Ray Stedman, *Body Life* (Glendale, Calif.: Regal Books, 1972), 63-64.

Chapter 1

1. Neal McBride, *How to Lead Small Groups* (Colorado Springs: NavPress, 1990), 26.

Chapter 2

1. Samuel Emerick, *Spiritual Renewal for Methodism* (Nashville: Methodist Evangelistic Materials, 1958), 8.

2. Ibid., 15.

3. Wood, "Directions and Cautions Addressed to Class Leaders," quoted in Emerick, *Spiritual Renewal for Methodism,* 25.

4. Emerick, *Spiritual Renewal for Methodism,* 1.

5. Ibid., 25-26.

6. Ibid., 30.

7. Ibid.

8. William Warren Sweet, *Methodism in American History* (Cincinnati: Methodist Book Concern, 1933], 332-33.

9. Emerick, *Spiritual Renewal for Methodism,* 44.

10. John Wesley, *Letters of John Wesley,* ed. John Telford (London: Epworth Press, 1936), 2:297.

Chapter 3

1. Taken from the book *We Really Do Need Each Other* (33-35), by Reuben Welch. Copyright © 1973 by Impact Books. Used by permission of Zondervan Publishing House.

2. "The Small Group Letter," *Discipleship Journal* 8, no. 6 (November-December 1988): 51. Used with permission.

3. W. Randolph Thornton, "Through Groups to God," *The Journal of Religious Education,* April 1957. Copyright Division of Christian Education of the National Council of Churches. Used with permission.

4. Sam Shoemaker, "So I Stay Near the Door," *Extraordinary Living for Ordinary Men* (Grand Rapids: Zondervan Publishing House, 1967), 140-42.

Chapter 4

1. James L. Garlow, *Partners in Ministry* (Kansas City: Beacon Hill Press of Kansas City, 1981), 54-55. Used by permission.

Chapter 5

1. Carl F. George, *Prepare Your Church for the Future* (Tarrytown, N.Y.: Fleming H. Revell, 1991), 87-88.

2. Dale E. Galloway, *20/20 Vision* (Portland, Oreg.: Scott Publishing, 1986), 140-42.

3. Karen Hurston and Judy Hamlin, "Three Basic Types of Small-Group Systems," *Discipleship Journal,* no. 62, March/April 1991, 43-44.

Chapter 6

1. Fletcher L. Byrom, quoted by John C. Maxwell on Injoy Tape Series (Bonita, Calif., 1993).

Chapter 7

1. Corrine Hamada Holmquist, "Plugging Kids into Your Small Group," *Discipleship Journal,* no. 78, November/December 1993, 115.

Chapter 9

1. Galloway, *20/20 Vision,* 17-22.

2. The author and publisher made a concerted effort to locate the owner or the owner's agent for permission to use this verse. Appropriate recognition of the owner and copyright holder, if known, will be included in any reprinting.

Chapter 10

1. Coleman, *The Master Plan of Evangelism,* 120.

2. Ibid., 107.

3. James Rutz, *The Open Church* (Auburn, Maine: The Seed Sowers, 1992), 35.

Chapter 11

1. The original, unaltered Twelve Steps of Alcoholics Anonymous read as follows:

> 1. We admitted we were powerless over alcohol—that our lives had become unmanageable.
>
> 2. We came to believe that a Power greater than ourselves could restore us to sanity.
>
> 3. We made a decision to turn our will and our lives over to the care of God as we understood Him.
>
> 4. We made a searching and fearless moral inventory of ourselves.
>
> 5. We admitted to God, to ourselves, and to another human being the exact nature of our wrongs.
>
> 6. We were entirely ready to have God remove all these defects of character.

7. We humbly asked Him to remove our shortcomings.

8. We made a list of all persons we had harmed and became willing to make amends to them all.

9. We made direct amends to such people wherever possible, except when to do so would injure them or others.

10. We continued to take personal inventory and, when we were wrong, promptly admitted it.

11. We sought through prayer and meditation to improve our conscious contact with God as we understood Him, praying only for knowledge of His will for us and the power to carry that out.

12. Having had a spiritual awakening as the result of these steps, we tried to carry this message to alcoholics and to practice these principles in all our affairs.

The Twelve Steps as listed in chapter 11 are reprinted and adapted with permission of Alcoholics Anonymous World Services, Inc. Permission to reprint and adapt this material does not mean that AA has reviewed or approved the contents of this publication, nor that AA agrees with the views expressed herein. AA is a program of recovery from alcoholism—use of the Twelve Steps in connection with programs and activities that are patterned after AA, but that address other problems, does not imply otherwise.

Chapter 12

1. Coleman, *The Master Plan of Evangelism,* 108.

2. Palmer Becker, *Called to Equip* (Scottdale, Pa.: Herald Press, 1993), 48.

3. Galloway, *20/20 Vision,* 132-33.

4. Ibid., 150-51.

Because the establishing of a network of small groups is a *process* and not another program, this ministry will be started before all the questions are answered. If you desire assistance with your small-group ministry, you may direct your correspondence to:

Pastor Floyd Schwanz
c/o Beacon Hill Press of Kansas City
P.O. Box 419527
Kansas City, MO 64141